Data Mining and Warehousing

Data Mining and Warehousing

S. Prabhu
N. Venkatesan

PUBLISHING FOR ONE WORLD

NEW AGE INTERNATIONAL (P) LIMITED, PUBLISHERS

New Delhi • Bangalore • Chennai • Cochin • Guwahati • Hyderabad
Jalandhar • Kolkata • Lucknow • Mumbai • Ranchi

Visit us at **www.newagepublishers.com**

Published by New Age International (P) Ltd., Publishers
First Edition: 2007
Reprint: 2026

GLOBAL OFFICES

• **New Delhi** **NEW AGE INTERNATIONAL (P) LIMITED, PUBLISHERS**
7/30 A, Daryaganj, New Delhi-110002, (INDIA), **Tel.:** (011) 23253472, 23253771, **Mob.:** 9315905300
E-mail: contactus@newagepublishers.com • Visit us at www.newagepublishers.com

• **London** **NEW AGE INTERNATIONAL (UK) LTD.**
27 Old Gloucester Street, London, WC1N 3AX, UK
E-mail: info@newacademicscience.co.uk • Visit us at www.newacademicscience.co.uk

BRANCHES

• **Bengaluru** 167, 1st Floor, 11th Cross, Mulkatamma Temple Road,Near Rajiv Gandhi Sports Complex, Vittal Nagar Bengaluru – 560026, **Tel.:** (080) 26756823, **Mob.:** 9315905288
E-mail: bangalore@newagepublishers.com

• **Chennai** 26, Damodaran Street, T. Nagar, Chennai-600 017, **Tel.:** (044) 24353401, **Mob.:** 9315905309
E-mail: chennai@newagepublishers.com

• **Cochin** CC-39/1016, Carrier Station Road, Ernakulam South, Cochin-682 016
Tel.: (0484) 4051304, **Mob.:** 9315905289, **E-mail: cochin@newagepublishers.com**

• **Guwahati** Hemsen Complex, Mohd. Shah Road, Paltan Bazar, Near Starline Hotel
Guwahati-781 008, **Tel.:** (0361) 2513881, **Mob.:** 9315905296, **E-mail: guwahati@newagepublishers.com**

• **Hyderabad** 105, 1st Floor, Madhiray Kaveri Tower, 3-2-19, Azam Jahi Road, Near Kumar Theater
Nimboliadda Kachiguda, Hyderabad-500 027, **Tel.:** (040) 24652456, **Mob.:** 9315905326
E-mail: hyderabad@newagepublishers.com

• **Kolkata** RDB Chambers (Formerly Lotus Cinema) 106A, 1st Floor, S N Banerjee Road
Kolkata-700 014, **Tel.:** (033) 22273773, **Mob.:** 9315905319, **E-mail: kolkata@newagepublishers.com**

• **Mumbai** 142C, Victor House, Ground Floor, N.M. Joshi Marg, Lower Parel, Mumbai-400 013
Tel.: (022) 24927869, 24915415, **Mob.:** 9315905282, **E-mail: mumbai@newagepublishers.com**

• **New Delhi** 22, Golden House, Daryaganj, New Delhi-110 002, **Tel.:** (011) 23262368, 23262370
Mob.: 9315905300, **E-mail: sales@newagepublishers.com**

Rs. 225/-

C-25-12-15205

Printed in India at Inkfinity Prints (P) Ltd., Noida.
Typeset at Vikas Computers, Delhi.

NEW AGE INTERNATIONAL (P) LIMITED, PUBLISHERS
7/30 A, Daryaganj, New Delhi - 110002
Visit us at **www.newagepublishers.com**
(CIN: U74899DL1966PTC004618)

Dedicated to our beloved *Grandparents...*

PREFACE

This book is intended as a text in data mining and warehousing for engineering and post-graduate level students.

We have attempted to cover the major topics in data mining and warehousing in depth. Advanced material, however, has been put into separate chapters so that courses in a variety of levels can be taught from this book. A brief synopsis of the chapters and comments on their appropriateness in a basic course is therefore appropriate.

Chapter 1 introduces the basic concepts to data mining and warehousing and its essentials.

Chapter 2 covers the types of knowledge and learning concepts, which are essential to data mining techniques.

Chapter 3 covers how to discover the knowledge hidden in the databases using various techniques.

Chapter 4 deals with various types of data mining techniques and algorithms available.

Chapter 5 covers various applications related to data mining techniques and real time usage of these techniques in various fields like business, commercial organizations, etc.

Chapter 6 deals with the evaluation of data warehouse and need of the new design process for databases.

Chapter 7 covers how to design the data warehouse using fact tables, dimension tables and schemas.

Chapter 8 deals with partitioning strategy in software and hardware.

Chapter 9 covers the data mart and meta data.

Chapter 10 covers backup and recovery process.

Chapter 11 deals with performance, tuning of data warehouse, challenges, benefits and new architecture of the data warehouse.

This book also contains sufficient material to make up an advanced course on data mining and warehousing. Each and every chapter has exercise. Model question paper is also given. We conclude that, this book is the only book, which deals both data mining techniques and data warehousing concepts suited for the modern time.

ACKNOWLEDGEMENT

Thanks and gratitude is owed to many kind individuals for their help in various ways in the completion of this book. Without such help, this book would indeed be poorer.

We first of all record our gratitude to the authorities of Bharathiyar College of Engineering and Technology, Karaikal, whose efforts maintained the progress of our work and ultimately put us in the right path.

Many experts made their contributions to the quality of writing by providing oversight and critiques in their special areas of interest. We particularly thank Dr. S.R. Rajagopalan, Ph.D., Retd. Scientist, N.A.L, Bangalore, for sparing his precious time in editing this book. We owe thanks to our colleagues and friends who have added to this book by providing us with their valuable suggestions. Such excellence as the book may have is owed in part to them, any errors are ours.

We are also indebted to our publishers Messrs. New Age International (P) Ltd. for their tolerance of our many requests and especially for their commitment to this book and its authors.

Once again we acknowledge our family members and wish them to know that our thanks are not merely "Proforma", they are sincerely offered and well deserved.

We particularly thank my graduate students for contributing a great deal to some of the original wording and editing.

And finally, each of us wishes to "doff his hat" to the other for the unstinting efforts to make this book the best possible, for the willingness to accept the advice of the other, and for the faith in our joint effort. We began writing this book an year ago as good friends and we completed it as even better friends.

S. Prabhu

N. Venkatesan

CONTENTS

CHAPTER 1

DATA MINING AND WAREHOUSING CONCEPTS

1.1 INTRODUCTION

The past couple of decades have seen a dramatic increase in the amount of information or data being stored in electronic format. This accumulation of data has taken place at an explosive rate. It has been estimated that the amount of information in the world doubles every 20 months and the sizes as well as number of databases are increasing even faster. There are many examples that can be cited. Point of sale data in retail, policy and claim data in insurance, medical history data in health care, financial data in banking and securities, are some instances of the types of data that is being collected.

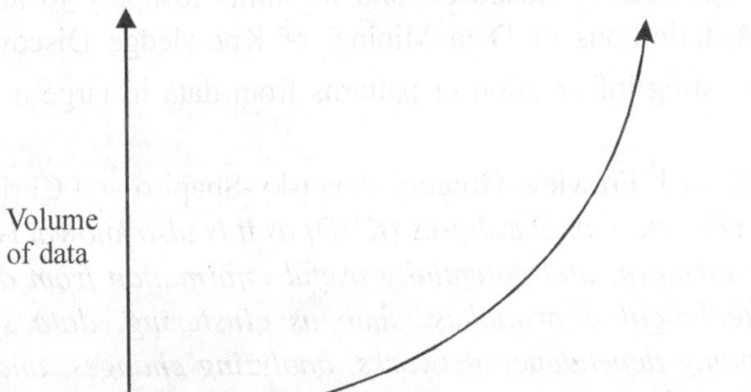

Fig. 1.1 The growing base of data

Data storage became easier as the availability of large amounts of computing power at low cost *i.e.*, the cost of processing power and storage is falling, made data cheap. There was also the introduction of new machine learning methods for knowledge representation based on logic programming etc. in addition to traditional statistical analysis of data. The new methods tend to be computationally intensive hence a demand for more processing power.

The *data storage* bits/bytes are calculated as follows:

✧ 1 byte = 8 bits

✧ 1 kilobyte (K/KB) = 2 ^ 10 bytes = 1,024 bytes

- 1 megabyte (M/MB) = 2 ^ 20 bytes = 1,048,576 bytes
- 1 gigabyte (G/GB) = 2 ^ 30 bytes = 1,073,741,824 bytes
- 1 terabyte (T/TB) = 2 ^ 40 bytes = 1,099,511,627,776 bytes
- 1 petabyte (P/PB) = 2 ^ 50 bytes = 1,125,899,906,842,624 bytes
- 1 exabyte (E/EB) = 2 ^ 60 bytes = 1,152,921,504,606,846,976 bytes
- 1 zettabyte (Z/ZB) =1 000 000 000 000 000 000 000 bytes
- 1 yottabyte (Y/YB) =1 000 000 000 000 000 000 000 000 bytes

It was recognized that information is at the heart of business operations and that decision-makers could make use of the data stored to gain valuable insight into the business. Database Management Systems gave access to the data stored but this was only a small part of what could be gained from the data. Traditional on-line transaction processing systems, OLTPs, are good at putting data into databases quickly, safely and efficiently but are not good at delivering meaningful analysis in return. Analyzing data can provide further knowledge about a business by going beyond the data explicitly stored to derive knowledge about the business. Data Mining, also called as data archeology, data dredging, data harvesting, is the process of extracting hidden knowledge from large volumes of raw data and using it to make crucial business decisions. This is where Data Mining or Knowledge Discovery in Databases (KDD) has obvious benefits for any enterprise.

1.2 DATA MINING DEFINITIONS

The term data mining has been stretched beyond its limits to apply to any form of data analysis. Some of the numerous definitions of Data Mining, or Knowledge Discovery in Databases are:

Extraction of interesting information or patterns from data in large databases is known as data mining.

According to William J. Frawley, Gregory Piatetsky-Shapiro and Christopher J. Matheus '*Data Mining, or Knowledge Discovery in Databases (KDD) as it is also known, is the nontrivial extraction of implicit, previously unknown, and potentially useful information from data. This encompasses a number of different technical approaches, such as clustering, data summarization, learning classification rules, finding dependency networks, analyzing changes, and detecting anomalies*'.

According to Marcel Holshemier and Arno Siebes "*Data mining is the search for relationships and global patterns that exist in large databases but are 'hidden' among the vast amount of data, such as a relationship between patient data and their medical diagnosis. These relationships represent valuable knowledge about the database and the objects in the database and, if the database is a faithful mirror, of the real world registered by the database*".

Data mining refers to "*using a variety of techniques to identify nuggets of information or decision-making knowledge in bodies of data, and extracting these in such a way that they can be put to use in the areas such as decision support, prediction, forecasting and estimation. The data is often voluminous, but as it stands of low value as no direct use can be made of it; it is the hidden information in the data that is useful*"

Data mining is concerned with the analysis of data and the use of software techniques for finding patterns and regularities in sets of data. It is the computer which is responsible for finding the patterns by identifying the underlying rules and features in the data. The idea is that it is possible to strike gold in unexpected places as the data mining software extracts patterns not previously discernable or so obvious that no-one has noticed them before.

Data mining analysis tends to work from the data up and the best techniques are those developed with an orientation towards large volumes of data, making use of as much of the collected data as possible to arrive at reliable conclusions and decisions. The analysis process starts with a set of data, uses a methodology to develop an optimal representation of the structure of the data during which time knowledge is acquired. Once knowledge has been acquired this can be extended to larger sets of data working on the assumption that the larger data set has a structure similar to the sample data. Again this is analogous to a mining operation where large amounts of low-grade materials are sifted through in order to find something of value.

1.3 DATA MINING TOOLS

The best of the best commercial database packages are now available for data mining and warehousing including IBM DB2, INFORMIX-On Line XPS, ORACLE9*i*, Clementine, Intelligent Miner, 4 Thought and SYBASE System 10.

1.3.1 Oracle Data Mining (ODM)

Oracle enables data mining inside the database for performance and scalability. Some of the capabilities are:

- ✧ An API that provides programmatic control and application integration
- ✧ Analytical capabilities with OLAP and statistical functions in the database
- ✧ Multiple Algorithms: Naïve Bayes and Association Rules
- ✧ Real-time and Batch Scoring modes
- ✧ Multiple Prediction types
- ✧ Association insights

ORACLE9*i* Data Mining provides a Java API to exploit the data mining functionality that is embedded within the ORACLE9*i* database. By delivering complete programmatic control of the database in data mining.

Oracle Data Mining (ODM) delivers powerful, scalable modeling and real-time scoring. This enables *e*-businesses to incorporate predictions and classifications in all processes and decision points throughout the business cycle.

ODM is designed to meet the challenges of vast amounts of data, delivering accurate insights completely integrated into *e*-business applications. This integrated intelligence enables the automation and decision speed that *e*-businesses require in order to compete today.

1.4 APPLICATIONS OF DATA MINING

Data mining has many and varied fields of application some of which are listed below.

1.4.1 Sales/Marketing

- ✧ Identify buying patterns from customers
- ✧ Find associations among customer demographic characteristics
- ✧ Predict response to mailing campaigns
- ✧ Market basket analysis

1.4.2 Banking

- ✧ Credit card fraudulent detection
- ✧ Identify 'loyal' customers
- ✧ Predict customers likely to change their credit card affiliation
- ✧ Determine credit card spending by customer groups
- ✧ Find hidden correlation's between different financial indicators
- ✧ Identify stock trading rules from historical market data

1.4.3 Insurance and Health Care

- ✧ Claims analysis *i.e.*, which medical procedures are claimed together
- ✧ Predict which customers will buy new policies
- ✧ Identify behaviour patterns of risky customers
- ✧ Identify fraudulent behaviour

1.4.4 Transportation

- ✧ Determine the distribution schedules among outlets
- ✧ Analyze loading patterns

1.4.5 Medicine

- ✧ Characterize patient behaviour to predict office visits
- ✧ Identify successful medical therapies for different illnesses

1.5 DATA WAREHOUSING AND CHARACTERISTICS

Data warehousing is a collection of *decision support* technologies, aimed at enabling the *knowledge worker* (executive, manager, analyst) to make better and faster decisions. Data mining potential can be enhanced if the appropriate data has been collected and stored in a data warehouse. A data warehouse is a relational database management system (RDBMS) designed specifically to meet the needs of transaction processing systems. It can be loosely defined as any centralized data repository which can be queried for business benefit but this will be more clearly defined later. Data warehousing is a new powerful technique making it possible to extract archived operational data and overcome inconsistencies between different legacy data formats. As well as integrating data throughout an enterprise, regardless of location, format, or communication requirements it is possible to incorporate additional or expert information.

In addition to a relational database, a data warehouse environment includes an extraction, transportation, transformation, and loading (ETL) solution, an online analytical processing (OLAP) engine, client analysis tools, and other applications that manage the process of gathering data and delivering it to business users.

ETL Tools are meant to extract, transform and load the data into Data Warehouse for decision making. Before the evolution of ETL Tools, the above mentioned ETL process was done manually by using SQL code created by programmers. This task was tedious in many cases since it involved many resources, complex coding and more work hours. On top of it, maintaining the code placed a great challenge among the programmers.

These difficulties are eliminated by ETL Tools since they are very powerful and they offer many advantages in all stages of ETL process starting from extraction, data cleansing, data profiling, transformation, debugging and loading into data warehouse when compared to the old method.

There are a number of ETL tools available in the market to do ETL process the data according to business/technical requirements. Following are some of those:

Tool name	*Company name*
Informatica	Informatica Corporation
DT/Studio	Embarcadero Technologies
Data Stage	IBM
Ab Initio	Ab Initio Software Corporation
Data Junction	Pervasive Software
Oracle Warehouse Builder	Oracle Corporation
Microsoft SQL Server Integration	Microsoft
Transform On Demand Solonde	ETL Solutions
Transformation Manager	

A common way of introducing data warehousing is to refer to the characteristics of a data warehouse as set forth by William Inmon, author of Building the Data Warehouse and the guru who is widely considered to be the originator of the data warehousing concept, is as follows:

- Subject Oriented
- Integrated
- Nonvolatile
- Time Variant

Data warehouses are designed to help you analyze data. For example, to learn more about your company's sales data, you can build a warehouse that concentrates on sales. Using this warehouse, you can answer questions like "Who was our best customer for this item last year?" This ability to define a data warehouse by subject matter, sales in this case, makes the data warehouse **subject oriented**.

Integration is closely related to subject orientation. Data warehouses must put data from disparate sources into a consistent format. They must resolve such problems as naming conflicts and inconsistencies among units of measure. When they achieve this, they are said to be **integrated**.

For instance, in one application, gender might be coded as "m" and "f" in another by 0 and 1. When data are moved from the operational environment into the data warehouse, they assume a consistent coding convention e.g. gender data is transformed to "m" and "f".

Nonvolatile means that, once entered into the warehouse, data should not change. This is logical because the purpose of a warehouse is to enable you to analyze what has occurred.

In order to discover trends in business, analysts need large amounts of data. This is very much in contrast to online transaction processing (OLTP) systems, where performance requirements demand that historical data be moved to an archive. A data warehouse's focus on change over time is what is meant by the term **time variant**. The data warehouse contains a place for storing data that are 10 to 20 years old, or older, to be used for comparisons, trends, and forecasting. These data are not updated.

1.6 DATA WAREHOUSE ARCHITECTURE

Data warehouse architecture includes tools for extracting data from multiple operational databases and external sources; for cleaning, transforming and integrating this data; for loading data into the data warehouse; and for periodically refreshing the warehouse to reflect updates at the sources and to purge data from the warehouse, perhaps onto slower archival storage. In addition to the main warehouse, there may be several departmental data marts. A data warehouse that is designed for a particular line of business, such as sales, marketing, or finance. In a dependent data mart, the data can be derived from an enterprise-wide data warehouse. In an independent data mart, data can be collected directly from sources. Data in the warehouse and data marts is stored and managed by

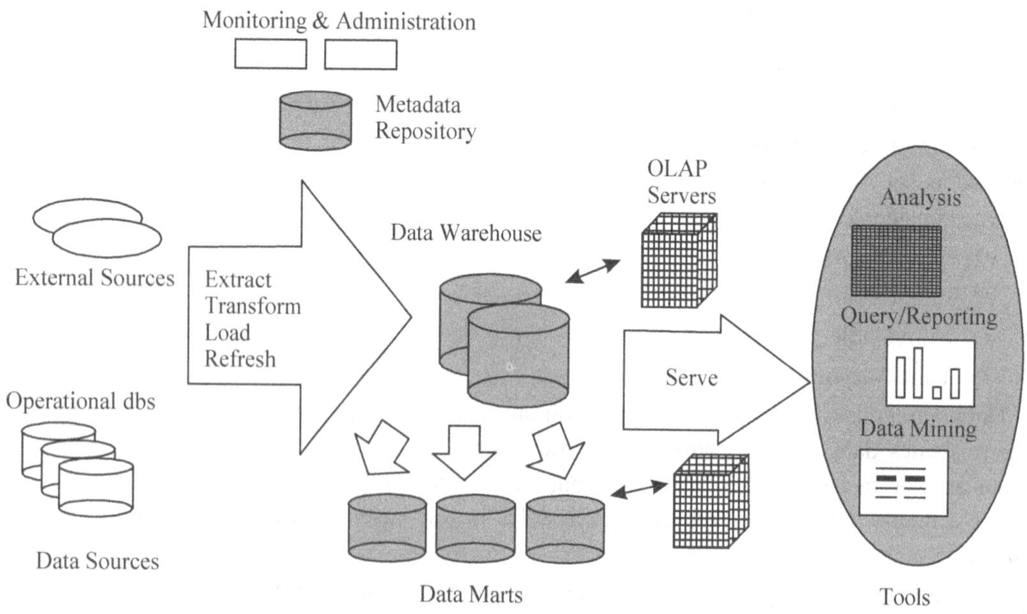

Fig. 1.2 Data warehousing architecture

one or more warehouse servers, which present multidimensional views of data to a variety of front end tools: query tools, report writers, analysis tools, and data mining tools. Finally, there is a repository for storing and managing meta data, and tools for monitoring and administering the warehousing system.

EXERCISE

1. Define data mining.
2. Explain the uses of data mining and describe any three data mining softwares.
3. What is data warehouse?
4. List out the characteristics of data warehouse.
5. Explain the data warehouse architecture.

CHAPTER 2

LEARNING AND TYPES OF KNOWLEDGE

2.1 INTRODUCTION

It seems that learning is one of the basic necessities of life; living creatures must have the ability to adapt themselves to their environment. There are undeniably many different ways of learning but instead of considering all kinds of different definitions, we will concentrate on an operational definition of the concept of learning, we will not state what learning is but rather specify how to determine when someone has learned something. In order to define learning operationally, we need two other concepts a certain 'task' to be carried out either well or badly and a learning 'subject' that is to carry out the task.

2.2 WHAT IS LEARNING?

An individual learns how to carry out a certain task by making a transition from a situation in which the task cannot be carried out to a situation in which the same task can be carried out under the same circumstances.

2.2.1 Inductive learning

Induction is the inference of information from data and inductive learning is the model building process where the environment *i.e.*, database is analyzed with a view to finding patterns. Similar objects are grouped in classes and rules formulated whereby it is possible to predict the class of unseen objects. This process of classification identifies classes such that each class has a unique pattern of values which forms the class description. The nature of the environment is dynamic hence the model must be adaptive *i.e.*, should be able to learn.

Generally it is only possible to use a small number of properties to characterize objects so we make abstractions in that objects which satisfy the same subset of properties are mapped to the same internal representation.

Inductive learning where the system infers knowledge itself from observing its environment has two main strategies:

- **Supervised learning**—This is learning from examples where a teacher helps the system construct a model by defining classes and supplying examples of each class. The system has to find a description of each class *i.e.*, the common properties in the examples. Once the description has been formulated the description and the class form a classification rule which can be used to predict the class of previously unseen objects. This is similar to discriminate analysis as in statistics.

✧ **Unsupervised learning**—This is learning from observation and discovery. The data mine system is supplied with objects but no classes are defined so it has to observe the examples and recognize patterns (*i.e.*, class description) by itself. This system results in a set of class descriptions, one for each class discovered in the environment. Again this similar to cluster analysis as in statistics.

Induction is therefore the extraction of patterns. The quality of the model produced by inductive learning methods is such that the model could be used to predict the outcome of future situations in other words not only for states encountered but rather for unseen states that could occur. The problem is that most environments have different states, *i.e.*, changes within, and it is not always possible to verify a model by checking it for all possible situations.

Given a set of examples the system can construct multiple models some of which will be simpler than others. The simpler models are more likely to be correct if we adhere to Ockham's razor, which states that if there are multiple explanations for a particular phenomenon it makes sense to choose the simplest because it is more likely to capture the nature of the phenomenon.

2.3 ANATOMY OF DATA MINING

The use of computer technology in decision support is now widespread and pervasive across a wide range of business and industry. This has resulted in the capture and availability of data in immense volume and proportion. There are many examples that can be cited. Point of sale data in retail, policy and claim data in insurance, medical history data in health care, financial data in banking and securities, are some instances of the types of data that is being collected. The data are typically a collection of records, where each individual record may correspond to a transaction or a customer, and the fields in the record correspond to attributes. Very often, these fields are of mixed type, with some being numerical (continuous valued, *e.g.*, age) and some symbolic (discrete valued, *e.g.*, disease).

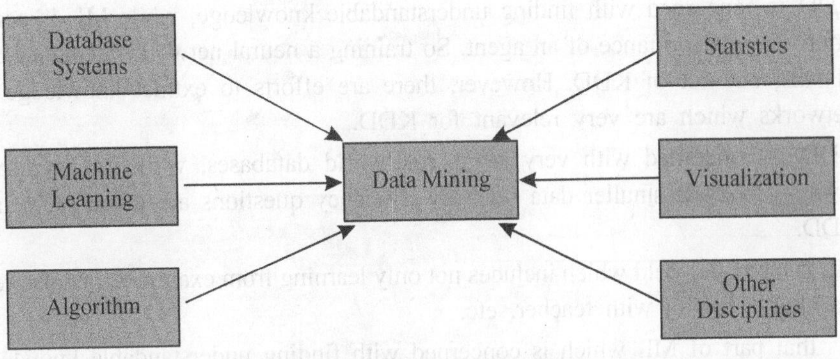

Fig. 2.1 Multi-disciplinary approach in data mining

2.3.1 Statistics

Statistics has a solid theoretical foundation but the results from statistics can be overwhelming and difficult to interpret as they require user guidance as to where and how to analyze the data. Data mining however allows the expert's knowledge of the data and the advanced analysis techniques of the computer to work together.

Analysts to detect unusual patterns and explain patterns using statistical models such as linear models have used statistical analysis systems such as SAS and SPSS. Statistics have a role to play and data mining will not replace such analyses but rather they can act upon more directed analyses based on the results of data mining. For example statistical induction is something like the average rate of failure of machines.

2.3.2 Machine Learning

Machine learning is the automation of a learning process and learning is tantamount to the construction of rules based on observations of environmental states and transitions. This is a broad field which includes not only learning from examples, but also reinforcement learning, learning with teacher, etc. A learning algorithm takes the data set and its accompanying information as input and returns a statement *e.g.*, a concept representing the results of learning as output. Machine learning examines previous examples and their outcomes and learns how to reproduce these and make generalizations about new cases.

Generally a machine learning system does not use single observations of its environment but an entire finite set called the training set at once. This set contains examples *i.e.*, observations coded in some machine readable form. The training set is finite hence not all concepts can be learned exactly.

2.3.2.1 Differences between Data Mining and Machine Learning

Knowledge Discovery in Databases (KDD) or Data Mining, and the part of Machine Learning (ML) dealing with learning from examples overlap in the algorithms used and the problems addressed.

The main differences are:

- KDD is concerned with finding understandable knowledge, while ML is concerned with improving performance of an agent. So training a neural network to balance a pole is part of ML, but not of KDD. However, there are efforts to extract knowledge from neural networks which are very relevant for KDD.
- KDD is concerned with very large, real-world databases, while ML typically (but not always) looks at smaller data sets. So efficiency questions are much more important for KDD.
- ML is a broader field which includes not only learning from examples, but also reinforcement learning, learning with teacher, etc.

KDD is that part of ML which is concerned with finding understandable knowledge in large sets of real-world examples. When integrating machine-learning techniques into database systems to implement KDD some of the databases require:

- More efficient learning algorithms because realistic databases are normally very large and noisy. It is usual that the database is often designed for purposes different from data mining and so properties or attributes that would simplify the learning task are not present nor can they be requested from the real world. Databases are usually contaminated by errors so the data mining algorithm has to cope with noise whereas ML has laboratory type examples *i.e.*, as near perfect as possible.
- More expressive representations for both data, *e.g.*, tuples in relational databases, which represent instances of a problem domain, and knowledge, *e.g.*, rules in a rule-based system, which can be used to solve users' problems in the domain, and the semantic information contained in the relational schemata.

Practical KDD systems are expected to include three interconnected phases

- Translation of standard database information into a form suitable for use by learning facilities;
- Using machine learning techniques to produce knowledge bases from databases; and
- Interpreting the knowledge produced to solve users' problems and/or reduce data spaces. //Data spaces being the number of examples.

2.3.3 Database Systems

A database is a collection of information related to a particular subject or purpose, such as tracking customer orders or maintaining a music collection.

2.3.4 Algorithms

2.3.4.1 Genetic Algorithms

Optimization techniques that use processes such as genetic combination, mutation, and natural selection in a design based on the concepts of natural evolution.

2.3.4.2 Statistical Algorithms

Statistics is the science of colleting, organizing, and applying numerical facts. Statistical analysis systems such as SAS and SPSS have been used by analysts to detect unusual patterns and explain patterns using statistical models such as linear models.

2.3.5 Visualization

Data visualization makes it possible for the analyst to gain a deeper, more intuitive understanding of the data and as such can work well along side data mining. Data mining allows the analyst to focus on certain patterns and trends and explore in-depth using visualization. On its own data visualization can be overwhelmed by the volume of data in a database but in conjunction with data mining can help with exploration. Visualization indicates the wide range of tool for presenting the reports to the end user .The presentation ranges from simple table to complex graph, using various 2D and 3D rendering techniques to distinguish information presented.

2.4 DIFFERENT TYPES OF KNOWLEDGE

Knowledge is a collection of interesting and useful pattern in a database.

The key issue in Knowledge Discovery in Database is to realize that there is more information hidden in your data than you are table to distinguish at first sight. In data mining we distinguish four different types of knowledge.

2.4.1 Shallow Knowledge

This is information that can be easily retrieved from database using a query tool such as Structured Query Language (SQL).

2.4.2 Multi-Dimensional Knowledge

OLAP tools you have the ability to rapidly explore all sorts of clusterings this is information that can be analyzed using online analytical processing tools. With and different orderings of the data but it is important to realize that most of the things you can do with an OLAP tool can also be done using SQL. The advantage of OLAP tools is that they are optimized for the kind of search and analysis operation. However, OLAP is not as powerful as data mining; it cannot search for optimal solutions.

2.4.3 Hidden Knowledge

This is data that can be found relative easily by using pattern recognition or machine learning algorithms. Again, one could use SQL to find these patterns but this would probably prove extremely time-consuming. A pattern recognition algorithm could find regularities in a database in minutes or at most a couple of hours, whereas you would have to spend months using SQL to achieve the same result. Here information that can be obtained through data mining techniques.

2.4.4 Deep Knowledge

This is information that is stored in the database but can only be located if we have a clue that tells us where to look. Hidden knowledge is the result of a search space over a gentle, hilly landscape; a search algorithm can easily find a reasonably optimal solution. Deep knowledge is typically the result of a search space over only a tiny local optimum, with no indication of any elevations in the neighborhood. A search algorithm could roam around this landscape for ever, without achieving any significant result. An example of this is encrypted information stored in a database. It is almost impossible to decipher a message that is encrypted if you do not have key, which indicates that, for the present at any rate, there is a limit to what one can learn.

TABLE 2.1 ***Different Types of Knowledge and Techniques***

Type of knowledge	*Technique*
Shallow knowledge	SQL
Multi-dimensional knowledge	OLAP
Hidden knowledge	Data mining
Deep knowledge	Clues

EXERCISE

1. What is learning? Explain different types of learning with example.
2. With a neat sketch explain the architecture of data mining.
3. What are the different kinds of knowledge?
4. Compare data mining with query tools.
5. Explain in detail about self-learning computer systems and concept learning.
6. Write in detail about data mining and query tools.
7. What are the differences between data mining and machine learning?

CHAPTER 3

KNOWLEDGE DISCOVERY PROCESS

3.1 INTRODUCTION

Data mining is an effective set of analysis tools and techniques used in the decision support process. However, misconceptions about the role that data mining plays in decision support solutions can lead to confusion about and misuse of these tools and techniques.

Data mining is not a "black box" process in which the data miner simply builds a data mining model and watches as meaningful information appears. Although Analysis Services removes much of the mystery and complexity of the data mining process by providing data mining tools for creating and examining data mining models, these tools work best on well-prepared data to answer well-researched business scenarios—the GIGO (garbage in, garbage out) law applies more to data mining than to any other area in Analysis Services. Quite a bit of work, including research, selection, cleaning, enrichment, and transformation of data, must be performed first if data mining is to truly supply meaningful information.

Data mining and data warehouses complement each other. Well-designed data warehouses have handled the data selection, cleaning, enrichment, and transformation steps that are also typically associated with data mining. Similarly, the process of data warehousing improves as, through data mining, it becomes apparent which data elements are considered more meaningful than others in terms of decision support and, in turn, improves the data cleaning and transformation steps that are so crucial to good data warehousing practices.

Data mining does not guarantee the behavior of future data through the analysis of historical data. Instead, data mining is a guidance tool, used to provide insight into the trends inherent in historical information.

Data mining, or Knowledge Discovery in Databases (KDD) as it is also known, is the nontrivial extraction of implicit, previously unknown, and potentially useful information from data. This encompasses a number of different technical approaches, such as clustering, data summarization, learning classification rules, finding dependency networks, analyzing changes, and detecting anomalies.

3.2 EVALUATION OF DATA MINING

TABLE 3.1 ***Data Mining Evaluation***

Evolutionary step	*Business question*	*Enabling technologies*	*Characteristics*
Data Collection (1960s)	"What was my total revenue in the last four years?"	Computers, tapes, disks	Retrospective, static data delivery.
Data Access (1980s)	"What were unit sales in New Delhi last May?"	Relational databases (RDBMS), Structured Query Language (SQL), ODBC	Retrospective, dynamic data delivery at record level.
Data Warehousing & Decision Support (1990s)	"What were unit sales in New Delhi last March? Drill down to Chennai."	On-line analytic processing (OLAP), multidimensional databases, data warehouses	Retrospective, dynamic data delivery at multiple levels.
Data Mining (Emerging Today)	"What's likely to happen to Chennai unit sales next month? Why?"	Advanced algorithms, multiprocessor computers, massive databases	Prospective, proactive information delivery.

3.3 STAGES OF THE DATA MINING PROCESS

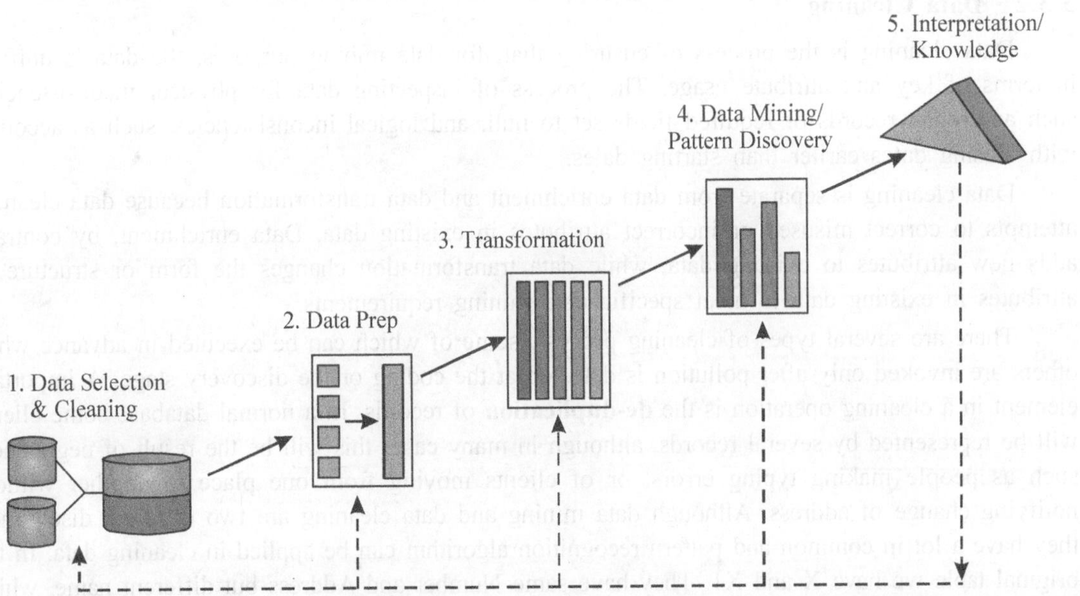

Fig. 3.1 An overview of the steps that compose the KDD process

3.3.1 Data Selection

There are two parts to selecting data for data mining. The first part, *locating data*, tends to be more mechanical in nature than the second part, *identifying data*, which requires significant input by a domain expert for the data.

A *domain expert* is someone who is intimately familiar with the business purposes and aspects, or *domain*, of the data to be examined.

In our example we start with a database containing records of patient for hypertension diseases with duration. It is a selection operational data from the Public Health Center patients of a small village contains information about the name, designation, age, address, disease particulars, period of diseases. In order to facilitate the KDD process, a copy of this operational data is drawn and stored in a separate database.

TABLE 3.2 *Original Data*

P.No.	*Name*	*Address*	*Sex*	*Age*	*Hype_dur*
101	U	UU1	Male	49	——
102	V	VV1	Male	45	10.5
103	W	WW1	Male	61	–10.5
104	X	XX1	Female	49	——
105	Y	YY1	Male	43	——
104	**XI**	XXI	Female	49	10.5

3.3.2 Data Cleaning

Data cleaning is the process of ensuring that, for data mining purposes, the data is uniform in terms of key and attribute usage. The process of inspecting data for physical inconsistencies, such as orphan records or required fields set to null, and logical inconsistencies, such as accounts with closing dates earlier than starting dates.

Data cleaning is separate from data enrichment and data transformation because data cleaning attempts to correct misused or incorrect attributes in existing data. Data enrichment, by contrast, adds new attributes to existing data, while data transformation changes the form or structure of attributes in existing data to meet specific data mining requirements.

There are several types of cleaning process, some of which can be executed in advance while others are invoked only after pollution is detected at the coding or the discovery stage. A important element in a cleaning operation is the **de-duplication** of records. In a normal database some clients will be represented by several records, although in many cases this will be the result of negligence, such as people making typing errors, or of clients moving from one place to another without notifying change of address. Although data mining and data cleaning are two different disciplines, they have a lot in common and pattern recognition algorithm can be applied in cleaning data. In the original table we have X and X1. They have same Number and Address but different name, which is a strong indication that they have the same person but that one of the spelling is incorrect.

TABLE 3.3 *De-duplication*

P.No.	*Name*	*Address*	*Sex*	*Age*	*Hype_dur*
101	U	UU1	Male	49	—
102	V	VV1	Male	45	10.5
103	W	WW1	Male	61	**-10.5**
104	X	XX1	Female	49	10.5
105	Y	YY1	Male	43	—

Second type of pollution that frequently occurs in lack of **domain consistency and disambiguation.** This type of pollution is particularly damaging, because it is hard to trace, but in greatly influence to type of patterns when we apply data mining to this table. In our example we replace the unknown data to NULL. The duration value is indicated in negative value for Patient number 103. The value must be positive so the incorrect value to be replaced with NULL.

TABLE 3.4 *Domain Consistency*

P.No.	*Name*	*Address*	*Sex*	*Age*	*Hype_dur*
101	U	UU1	Male	49	NULL
102	V	VV1	Male	45	10.5
103	W	WW1	Male	61	NULL
104	X	XX1	Female	49	10.5
105	Y	YY1	Male	43	NULL

3.3.3 Data Enrichment

Data enrichment is the process of adding new attributes, such as calculated fields or data from external sources, to existing data. Most references on data mining tend to combine this step with data transformation. Data transformation involves the manipulation of data, but data enrichment involves adding information to existing data. This can include combining internal data with external data, obtained from either different departments or companies or vendors that sell standardized industry-relevant data.

Data enrichment is an important step if you are attempting to mine marginally acceptable data. You can add information to such data from standardized external industry sources to make the data mining process more successful and reliable, or provide additional derived attributes for a better understanding of indirect relationships. For example, data warehouses frequently provide pre aggregation across business lines that share common attributes for cross-selling analysis purposes.

As with data cleaning and data transformation, this step is best handled in a temporary storage area. Data enrichment, in particular the combination of external data sources with data to be mined, can require a number of updates to both data and meta data, and such updates are generally not acceptable in an established data warehouse.

In our example, we will suppose that we have purchased extra information about our patients consisting of age, kidney, heart and stroke related disease. This is more realistic than it may initially seen, since it is quite possible to buy demographic data on average age for a certain neighborhood and hypertension and diabetes patients can be traced fairly easily. For this, however, it is not particularly important how the information was gathered and be easily be joined to the existing records.

TABLE 3.5 ***Enrichment***

Name	*Address*	*Sex*	*Age*	*Kidney*	*Heart*	*Stroke*
U	UU1	Male	49	No	Yes	No
V	VV1	Male	45	No	Yes	No
W	WW1	Male	61	No	Yes	No
X	XX1	Female	49	No	Yes	No
Y	YY1	Male	43	No	No	No

3.3.4 Data Transformation

Data transformation, in terms of data mining, is the process of changing the form or structure of existing attributes. Data transformation is separate from data cleansing and data enrichment for data mining purposes because it does not correct existing attribute data or add new attributes, but instead grooms existing attributes for data mining purposes.

3.3.5 Coding

That data in our example can undergo a number of transformations. First the extra information that was purchased to enrich the database is added to the records describing the individuals.

In our example we convert disease yes-no into 1 and 0. In the next stage, we select only those records that have enough information to be of value. Although it is difficult to give detailed rules for this kind of operation, this is a situation that occurs frequently in practice. In most tables that are collected from operational data, a lot of desirable data is missing and most is impossible to retrieve. A general rule states that any detection of data must be a conscious decision, after a thorough analysis of the possible consequences. In some cases, especially fraud detection, lack of information can be a valuable indication of interesting patterns.

TABLE 3.6 ***Coded Database***

Name	*Occupation*	*Address*	*Sex*	*Age*	*HypeDur*	*Diadur*	*Kidney*	*Heart*	*Stroke*	*HyperTension*	*Diabetes*
U	Labor	UU1	Male	49	NULL	NULL	0	1	0	1	0
V	Farmer	VV1	Male	45	10.5	13	0	1	0	0	1
W	Farmer	WW1	Male	61	NULL	14	0	1	0	0	1
X	Farmer	XX1	Female	49	10.5	15	0	1	0	1	0
Y	Farmer	YY1	Male	43	NULL	NULL	0	0	0	1	0

TABLE 3.7 ***Final Table after Removing Rows***

Name	Occupation	Address	Sex	Age	HypeDur (Years)	Diadur (Years)	Kidney	Heart	Stroke	HyperTension	Diabetes
V	Farmer	VV1	Male	45	10.5	13	0	1	0	0	1
X	Farmer	XX1	Female	49	10.5	15	0	1	0	1	0

3.3.6 Data Mining

The discovery stage of the KDD process is fascinating. Here we shall discuss some of the most important machine-learning and pattern recognition algorithms, and in this way get an idea of the opportunities that are available as well as some of the problems that occur during the discovery stage. We shall see that some learning algorithms do well on one part of the set where others fail, and this clearly indicates the need for hybrid learning. We shall also show that there is a relationship is detected during the data mining stage.

Data mining is not so much a single technique as the idea that there is more knowledge hidden in the data than shows itself on the surface. From this point of view, data mining is really an 'anything goes' affair. Any technique that helps extract more out of our data in useful, so data mining techniques from quite a heterogeneous group. Although various different techniques are used for different purposes, those that are of interest in present context are:

- ✧ Query tools
- ✧ Statistical techniques
- ✧ Visualization
- ✧ Online analytical processing
- ✧ Case based learning (*k*-nearest neighbor)
- ✧ Decision trees
- ✧ Association rules
- ✧ Neural networks
- ✧ Genetic algorithms

3.3.7 Visualization/Interpretation/Evaluation

Visualization techniques are a very useful method of discovering patterns in datasets, and may be used at the beginning of a data mining process to get a rough feeling of the quality of the data set and where patterns are to be found. Interesting possibilities are offered by object oriented three dimensional tool kits, such as Inventor, which enable to user to explore three dimensional structures interactively. Advanced graphical techniques in virtual reality enable people to wander through artificial data spaces, white historic development of data sets can be displayed as a kind of animated movie. These simple methods can provide us with a wealth of information. An elementary technique that can be of great value is the so called scatter diagram. Scatter diagrams can be used to identify interesting subsets of the data sets so that we can focus on the rest of the data mining process. There is a whole field of research dedicated to the search for interesting projections for data sets-that is called projection pursuit.

3.4 DATA MINING OPERATIONS

Four operations are associated with discovery-driven data mining.

3.4.1 Creation of Prediction and Classification Models

This is the most commonly used operation primarily because of the proliferation of automatic model development techniques. The goal of this operation is to use the contents of the database, which reflect historical data, *i.e.*, data about the past, to automatically generate a model that can predict a future behavior. Model creation has been traditionally pursued using statistical techniques. The value added by data mining techniques in this operation is in their ability to generate models that are comprehensible, and explainable, since many data mining modeling techniques express models as sets of if... then... rules.

3.4.2 Association

Whereas the goal of the modeling operation is to create a generalized description that characterizes the contents of a database, the goal of Association is to establish relations between the records in a data base.

3.4.3 Database Segmentation

As databases grow and are populated with diverse types of data it is often necessary to partition them into collections of related records either as a means of obtaining a summary of each database, or before performing a data mining operation such as model creation.

3.4.4 Deviation Detection

This operation is the exact opposite of database segmentation. In particular, its goal is to identify outlying points in a particular data set, and explain whether they are due to noise or other impurities being present in the data, or due to causal reasons. It is usually applied in conjunction with database segmentation. It is usually the source of true discovery since outliers express deviation from some previously known expectation and norm.

3.5 ARCHITECTURE OF DATA MINING

Based on databases, data warehouse of a typical data mining system may have the following components.

Database, data warehouse or other information repository

This is one or a set of databases, data warehouses, spreadsheets or other kinds of information repositories. Data cleaning and data integration techniques may be performed on the data.

Database or data warehouse server

The database or data warehouse server is responsible for fetching the relevant data, based on the user's data mining request.

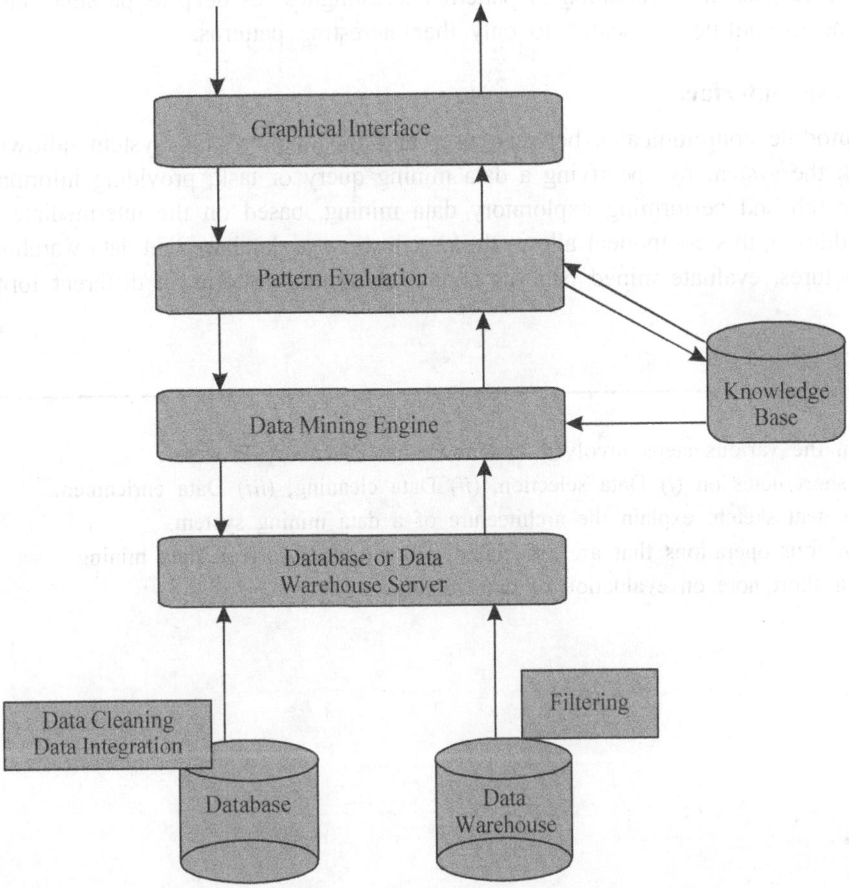

Fig. 3.2 Architecture of data mining

Knowledge base

This is the domain knowledge that is used to guide the search or evaluate the interestingness of resulting patterns. Such knowledge can include concept hierarchies, used to organize attributes or attribute values into different levels of abstraction. Knowledge such as user beliefs, which can be used to assess a pattern's interestingness based on its unexpectedness, may also be included.

Data mining engine

This is essential to the data mining system and ideally consists of a set of functional modules for tasks such as characterization, association, classification, cluster analysis and evolution and deviation analysis.

Pattern evaluation module

This component typically employs interestingness measures and interacts with the data mining modules so as to focus the search towards interesting patterns. For efficient data mining, it is highly recommended to push the evaluation of pattern interestingness as deep as possible into the mining process so as to confine the search to only the interesting patterns.

Graphical user interface

This module communicates between user and the data mining system, allowing the user interact with the system by specifying a data mining query or task, providing information to help focus the search and performing exploratory data mining, based on the intermediate data mining results. In addition, this component allows the user to browse database and data warehouse schemes or data structures, evaluate mined patterns and visualize the patterns in different forms.

EXERCISE

1. Explain the various steps involved in Knowledge Discovery Process.
2. Write short notes on (*i*) Data selection, (*ii*) Data cleaning, (*iii*) Data enrichment.
3. With a neat sketch, explain the architecture of a data mining system.
4. Explain four operations that are associated with discovery-driven data mining.
5. Write a short note on evaluation of data mining.

CHAPTER 4

DATA MINING TECHNIQUES

4.1 INTRODUCTION

There are several different methods used to perform data mining tasks. These techniques not only require specific types of data structures, but also imply certain types of algorithmic approaches. In this chapter, we briefly examined some of the data mining techniques.

4.2 CLASSIFICATION

Classification is learning a function that maps a data item into one of several predefined classes. Examples of classification methods used as part of knowledge discovery applications include classifying trends in financial markets and automated identification of *objects of interest in large image* databases. *Prediction* involves using some variables or fields in the database to predict unknown or future values of other variables of interest. *Description* focuses on finding human interpretable patterns describing the data.

4.3 NEURAL NETWORKS

Neural Networks are analytic techniques modeled after the (hypothesized) processes of learning in the cognitive system and the neurological functions of the brain and capable of predicting new

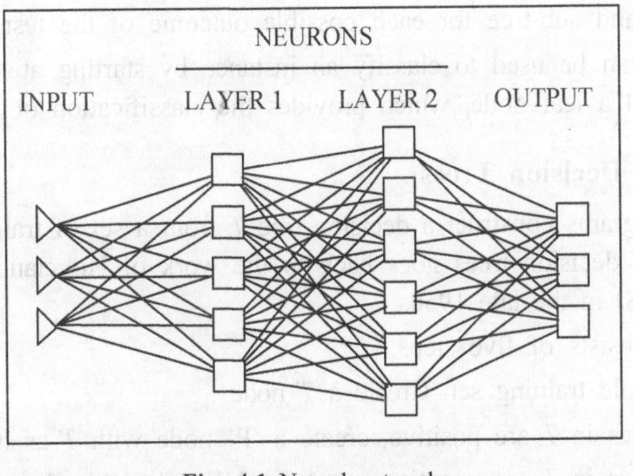

Fig. 4.1 Neural networks

observations (on specific variables) from other observations (on the same or other variables) after executing a process of so-called learning from existing data.

The neural network is then subjected to the process of "training." In that phase, neurons apply an iterative process to the number of inputs (variables) to adjust the weights of the network in order to optimally predict (in traditional terms one could say, find a "fit" to) the sample data on which the "training" is performed. After the phase of learning from an existing data set, the neural network is ready and it can then be used to generate predictions.

Neural Networks techniques can also be used as a component of analyses designed to build explanatory models because *Neural Networks* can help explore data sets in search for relevant variables or groups of variables; the results of such explorations can then facilitate the process of model building.

Advantages

Neural Networks is that, theoretically, they are capable of approximating any continuous function, and thus the researcher does not need to have any hypotheses about the underlying model, or even to some extent, which variables matter.

Disadvantages

The final solution depends on the initial conditions of the network. It is virtually impossible to "interpret" the solution in traditional, analytic terms, such as those used to build theories that explain phenomena.

4.4 DECISION TREES

Decision trees are powerful and popular tools for classification and prediction. Decision trees represent *rules*. *Decision tree* is a classifier in the form of a tree structure where each node is either:

- a *leaf node*, indicating a class of instances, or
- a *decision node* that specifies some test to be carried out on a single attribute value, with one branch and sub-tree for each possible outcome of the test.

A decision tree can be used to classify an instance by starting at the root of the tree and moving through it until a leaf node, which provides the classification of the instance.

4.4.1 Constructing Decision Trees

Decision tree programs construct a decision tree T from a set of training cases. The original idea of construction of decision trees goes back to the work of Hoveland and Hunt on *Concept Learning Systems* (CLS) in the late 1950s.

The algorithm consists of five steps.

1. $T \leftarrow$ the whole training set. Create a T node.
2. If all examples in T are positive, create a 'P' node with T as its parent and stop.
3. If all examples in T are negative, create a 'N' node with T as its parent and stop.

4. Select an attribute X with values v_1, v_2, ..., v_N and partition T into subsets T_1, T_2, ..., T_N according their values on X. Create N nodes T_i (i = 1,...., N) with T as their parent and $X = v_i$ as the label of the branch from T to T_i.
5. For each T_i do: $T \leftarrow T_i$ and go to step 2.

Example for decision tree

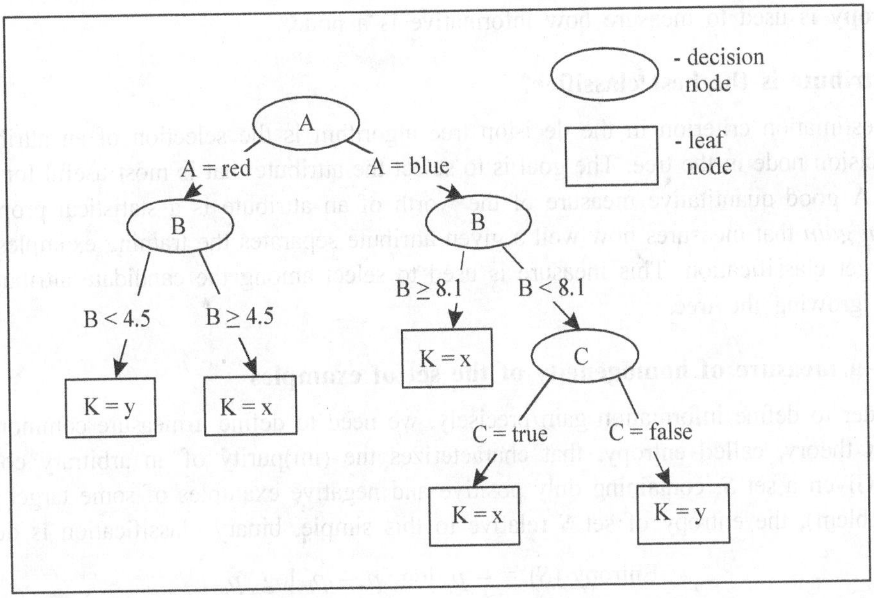

Fig. 4.2 An example of a simple decision tree

Decision tree induction is a typical inductive approach to learn knowledge on classification. The key requirements to do mining with decision trees are:

Predefined classes: The categories to which cases are to be assigned must have been established beforehand (supervised data).

Discrete classes: A case does or does not belong to a particular class, and there must be for more cases than classes.

Sufficient data: Usually hundreds or even thousands of training cases.

"Logical" classification model: Classifier that can be only expressed as decision trees or set of production rules.

4.4.2 ID3 Decision Tree Algorithm

J. Ross Quinlan originally developed ID3 at the University of Sydney. He first presented ID3 in 1975 in a book, *Machine Learning*, vol. 1, no. 1. ID3 is based on the Concept Learning System (CLS) algorithm.

4.4.2.1 Basic Ideas Behind ID3

In the decision tree each node corresponds to a non-goal attribute and each arc to a possible value of that attribute.

A leaf of the tree specifies the expected value of the goal attribute for the records described by the path from the root to that leaf. [This defines what a decision tree is.]

In the decision tree at each node should be associated the non-goal attribute which is **most informative** among the attributes not yet considered in the path from the root.

Entropy is used to measure how informative is a node.

Which attribute is the best classifier?

The estimation criterion in the decision tree algorithm is the selection of an attribute to test at each decision node in the tree. The goal is to select the attribute that is most useful for classifying examples. A good quantitative measure of the worth of an attribute is a statistical property called *information gain* that measures how well a given attribute separates the training examples according to their target classification. This measure is used to select among the candidate attributes at each step while growing the tree.

Entropy—a measure of homogeneity of the set of examples

In order to define information gain precisely, we need to define a measure commonly used in information theory, called entropy, that characterizes the (im)purity of an arbitrary collection of examples. Given a set S, containing only positive and negative examples of some target concept (a 2 class problem), the entropy of set S relative to this simple, binary classification is defined as:

$$\text{Entropy }(S) = -\,p_p \log_2 p_p - p_n \log_2 p_n$$

where p_p is the proportion of positive examples in S and p_n is the proportion of negative examples in S. In all calculations involving entropy we define 0log0 to be 0.

To illustrate, suppose S is a collection of 25 examples, including 15 positive and 10 negative examples [15+, 10–]. Then the entropy of S relative to this classification is

$$\text{Entropy }(S) = -\,(15/25) \log_2 (15/25) - (10/25) \log_2 (10/25) = 0.970$$

Notice that the entropy is 0 if all members of S belong to the same class. For example, if all members are positive ($p_p = 1$), then p_n is 0, and Entropy $(S) = -1' \log_2(1) - 0' \log_2 0 = -1' \; 0 - 0' \log_2 0 = 0$. Note the entropy is 1 (at its maximum!) when the collection contains an equal number of positive and negative examples. If the collection contains unequal numbers of positive and negative examples, the entropy is between 0 and 1. Fig. 4.3 shows the form of the entropy function relative to a binary classification, as p_+ varies between 0 and 1.

One interpretation of entropy from information theory is that it specifies the minimum number of bits of information needed to encode the classification of an arbitrary member of S (*i.e.*, a member of S drawn at random with uniform probability). For example, if p_p is 1, the receiver knows the drawn example will be positive, so no message need be sent, and the entropy is 0. On the other hand, if p_p is 0.5, one bit is required to indicate whether the drawn example is positive or negative.

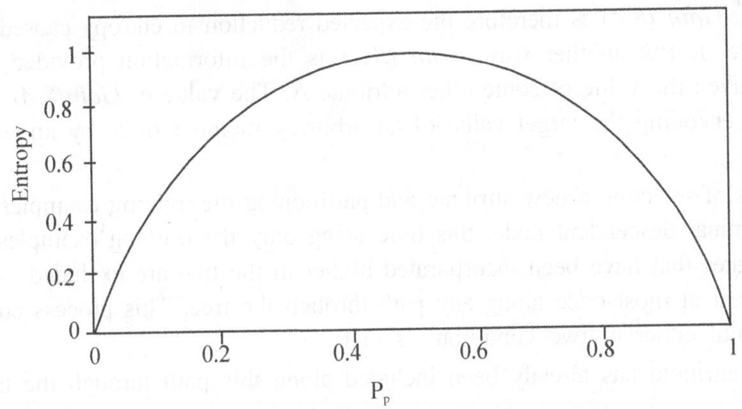

Fig. 4.3 The entropy function relative to a binary classification, as the proportion of positive examples p_p varies between 0 and 1

If p_p is 0.8, then a collection of messages can be encoded using on average less than 1 bit per message by assigning shorter codes to collections of positive examples and longer codes to less likely negative examples.

Thus far we have discussed entropy in the special case where the target classification is binary. If the target attribute takes on *c* different values, then the entropy of *S* relative to this *c*-wise classification is defined as

$$\text{Entropy}(S) = \sum_{i=1}^{c} - p_i \log_2 p_i$$

where p_i is the proportion of *S* belonging to class *i*. Note the logarithm is still base 2 because entropy is a measure of the expected encoding length measured in bits. Note also that if the target attribute can take on *c* possible values, the maximum possible entropy is $\log_2 c$.

Information gain measures the expected reduction in entropy

Given entropy as a measure of the impurity in a collection of training examples, we can now define a measure of the effectiveness of an attribute in classifying the training data. The measure we will use, called *information gain,* is simply the expected reduction in entropy caused by partitioning the examples according to this attribute. More precisely, the information gain, *Gain* (*S*, *A*) of an attribute *A*, relative to a collection of examples *S*, is defined as

$$\text{Gain}(S, A) = \text{Entropy}(S) - \sum_{v \in \text{Values}(A)} \frac{|S_v|}{|S|} \text{Entropy}(S_v)$$

where *Values(A)* is the set of all possible values for attribute *A*, and S_v is the subset of *S* for which attribute *A* has value *v* (*i.e.*, $S_v = \{s \in S \mid A(s) = v\}$). Note the first term in the equation for *Gain* is just the entropy of the original collection *S* and the second term is the expected value of the entropy after *S* is partitioned using attribute *A*. The expected entropy described by this second term is simply the sum of the entropies of each subset S_v, weighted by the fraction of examples $|S_v|/|S|$

that belong to S_v. *Gain (S,A)* is therefore the expected reduction in entropy caused by knowing the value of attribute *A*. Put another way, *Gain (S,A)* is the information provided about the target attribute value, given the value of some other attribute A. The value of *Gain(S,A)* is the number of bits saved when encoding the target value of an arbitrary member of *S*, by knowing the value of attribute *A*.

The process of selecting a new attribute and partitioning the training examples is now repeated for each non-terminal descendant node, this time using only the training examples associated with that node. Attributes that have been incorporated higher in the tree are excluded, so that any given attribute can appear at most once along any path through the tree. This process continues for each new leaf node until either of two conditions is met:

1. Every attribute has already been included along this path through the tree, or
2. the training examples associated with this leaf node all have the same target attribute value (*i.e.*, their entropy is zero).

Algorithm

```
function ID3
Input: (R: a set of non-target attributes,
        C: the target attribute,
        S: a training set) returns a decision tree;
begin
  If S is empty, return a single node with value failure;
  If S consists of records all with the same
     value for the target attribute,
     return a single leaf node with that value;
  If R is empty, then return a single node with
     the value of the most frequent of the values of the
     target attribute that are found in records of S; [in that case
     there may be errors, examples that will be improperly classified];
  Let A be the attribute with largest Gain(A,S) among attributes in R;
  Let {Aj| j=1,2, .., m} be the values of attribute A;
  Let {Sj| j=1,2, .., m} be the subsets of S consisting
     respectively of records with value aj for A;
  Return a tree with root labeled A and arcs
     labeled a1, a2, .., am going respectively
     to the trees (ID3(R-{A}, C, S1), ID3(R-{A}, C, S2),
     .....,ID3(R-{A}, C, Sm);
  Recursively apply ID3 to subsets {Sj| j=1,2, .., m}
     until they are empty
end.
```

Example of ID3

Suppose we want ID3 to decide whether the weather is amenable to playing cricket. Over the course of 2 weeks, data is collected to help ID3 build a decision tree (see Table 4.2). The target classification is "should we play cricket" which can be yes or no. The weather attributes are outlook, temperature, humidity, and wind speed. They can have the following values:

outlook = {sunny, overcast, rain}

temperature = {hot, mild, cool}

humidity = {high, normal}

wind = {weak, strong}

Examples of set *S* are:

TABLE 4.2 *Weather Report*

Day	*Outlook*	*Temperature*	*Humidity*	*Wind*	*Play ball*
D1	Sunny	Hot	High	Weak	No
D2	Sunny	Hot	High	Strong	No
D3	Overcast	Hot	High	Weak	Yes
D4	Rain	Mild	High	Weak	Yes
D5	Rain	Cool	Normal	Weak	Yes
D6	Rain	Cool	Normal	Strong	No
D7	Overcast	Cool	Normal	Strong	Yes
D8	Sunny	Mild	High	Weak	No
D9	Sunny	Cool	Normal	Weak	Yes
D10	Rain	Mild	Normal	Weak	Yes
D11	Sunny	Mild	Normal	Strong	Yes
D12	Overcast	Mild	High	Strong	Yes
D13	Overcast	Hot	Normal	Weak	Yes
D14	Rain	Mild	High	Strong	No

If *S* is a collection of 14 examples with 9 YES and 5 NO examples then,

$$\text{Entropy}(S) = -(9/14)\ \text{Log2}\ (9/14) - (5/14)\ \text{Log2}\ (5/14) = 0.940$$

Notice entropy is 0 if all members of *S* belong to the same class (the data is perfectly classified). The range of entropy is 0 ("perfectly classified") to 1 ("totally random").

Gain(*S*, *A*) is information gain of example set *S* on attribute *A* is defined as

$$\text{Gain}(S, A) = \text{Entropy}(S) - \Sigma\ ((|S_v|/|S|) * \text{Entropy}(S_v))$$

Where:

Σ = value v of all possible values of attribute A

S_v = subset of S for which attribute A has value v

$|S_v|$ = number of elements in S_v

$|S|$ = number of elements in S.

Suppose *S* is a set of 14 examples in which one of the attributes is wind speed. The values of Wind can be *Weak* or *Strong*. The classification of these 14 examples are 9 YES and 5 NO. For attribute Wind, suppose there are 8 occurrences of Wind = Weak and 6 occurrences of Wind = Strong. For Wind = Weak, 6 of the examples are YES and 2 are NO. For Wind = Strong, 3 are YES and 3 are NO. Therefore,

Gain(S,Wind) = Entropy(S)–(8/14)*Entropy(S_{weak})–(6/14)*Entropy(S_{strong})

= 0.940 – (8/14)*0.811 – (6/14)*1.00 = 0.048

Entropy(S_{weak}) = – (6/8)*log2(6/8) – (2/8)*log2(2/8) = 0.811

Entropy(S_{strong}) = – (3/6)*log2(3/6) – (3/6)*log2(3/6) = 1.00

For each attribute, the gain is calculated and the highest gain is used in the decision node.

We need to find which attribute will be the root node in our decision tree. The gain is calculated for all four attributes:

Gain(S, Outlook) = 0.246

Gain(S, Temperature) = 0.029

Gain(S, Humidity) = 0.151

Gain(S, Wind) = 0.048

Outlook attribute has the highest gain, therefore it is used as the decision attribute in the root node.

Since Outlook has three possible values, the root node has three branches (sunny, overcast, rain). The next question is "what attribute should be tested at the Sunny branch node?" Since we have used Outlook at the root, we only decide on the remaining three attributes: Humidity, Temperature, or Wind.

S_{sunny} = {D1, D2, D8, D9, D11} = 5 examples from Table 1 with outlook = sunny

Gain(S_{sunny}, Humidity) = 0.970

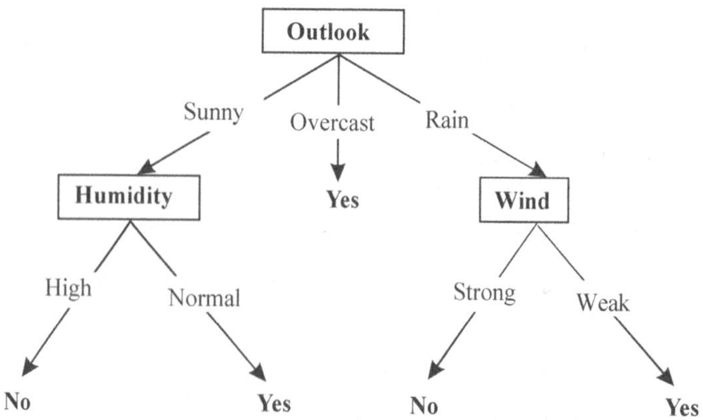

Fig. 4.4 A decision tree for the concept *Playball*

Gain(S_{sunny}, Temperature) = 0.570

Gain(S_{sunny}, Wind) = 0.019

Humidity has the highest gain; therefore, it is used as the decision node. This process goes on until all data is classified perfectly or we run out of attributes.

The final decision = tree

The decision tree can also be expressed in rule format:

IF outlook = sunny AND humidity = high THEN cricket = no

IF outlook = rain AND humidity = high THEN cricket = no

IF outlook = rain AND wind = strong THEN cricket = yes

IF outlook = overcast THEN cricket = yes

IF outlook = rain AND wind = weak THEN cricket = yes.

ID3 has been incorporated in a number of commercial rule-induction packages. Some specific applications include medical diagnosis, credit risk assessment of loan applications, equipment malfunctions by their cause, classification of soybean diseases, and web search classification.

4.4.4 A Detailed Survey on Decision Tree Technique

A decision tree contains zero or more internal nodes and one or more leaf nodes.

All internal nodes have two or more child nodes.

All non-terminal nodes contain splits, which test the value of a mathematical or logical expression of the attributes.

Each leaf node has a class label associated with it.

The task of constructing a tree from the training set is called tree induction.

4.4.5 Appropriate Problems for Decision Tree Learning

Instances are represented by **attribute-value pairs.**

Instances are described by a fixed set of attributes (*e.g.*, temperature) and their values (*e.g.*, hot).

The easiest situation for decision tree learning occurs when each attribute takes on a small number of disjoint possible values (*e.g.*, hot, mild, cold).

4.4.6 Decision Tree Algorithms

Name of the Algorithm	*Developer*	*Year*
CHAID	Kass	1980
CART	Breimarn, *et al.*	1984
ID3	Quinlan	1986
C4.5	Quinlan	1993
SLIQ	Agrawal, *et al.*	1996
SPRINT	Agrawal, *et al.*	1996

4.4.7 Strengths and Weaknesses of Decision Tree Methods

The strengths of decision tree methods

1. Decision trees are able to generate understandable rules.
2. Decision trees perform classification without requiring much computation.
3. Decision trees are able to handle both continuous and categorical variables.
4. Decision trees provide a clear indication of which fields are most important for prediction or classification.

The weaknesses of decision tree methods

Decision trees are less appropriate for estimation tasks where the goal is to predict the value of a continuous variable such as income, blood pressure, or interest rate. Decision trees are also problematic for time-series data unless a lot of effort is put into presenting the data in such a way that trends and sequential patterns are made visible.

1. Error-Prone with Too Many Classes.
2. Computationally Expensive to Train.
3. Trouble with Non-Rectangular Regions.

4.5 GENETIC ALGORITHM

Genetic Algorithms/Evolutionary algorithms are based on Darwin's theory of survival of the fittest. Here the best program or logic survives from a pool of solutions. Two programs called chromosomes combine to produce a third program called child, the reproduction process goes through Crossover and Mutation operations.

4.5.1 Crossover

Using simple single point crossover reproduction mechanism, a point along the chromosome length is randomly chosen at which the crossover is done as illustrated.

(*a*) Single Point Crossover: In this type, one crossover point is selected and the string from the beginning of chromosome to the crossover point is copied from one parent and the rest is copied from the second parent resulting in a child. For instance, consider the following chromosomes and crossover point at position 4.

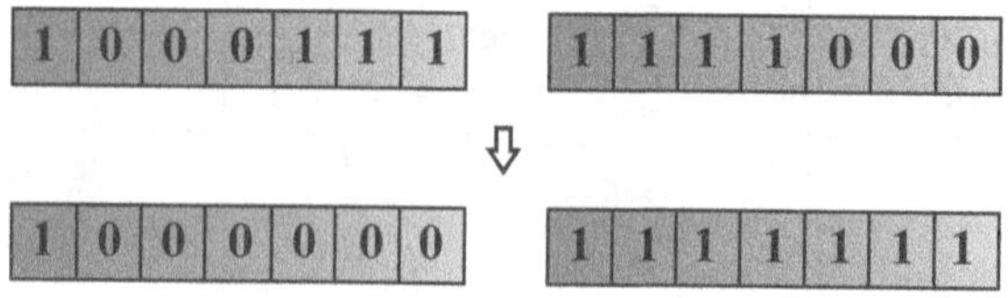

Fig. 4.5 Single point crossover

Here we observe that the regions after the crossover point are interchanged in the children.

***(b)* Two Point Crossover:** In this type, two crossover points are selected and the string from beginning of one chromosome to the first crossover point is copied from one parent, the part from the first to the second crossover point is copied from the second parent and the rest is copied from the first parent. This type of crossover is mainly employed in permutation encoding and value encoding where a single point crossover would result in inconsistencies in the child chromosomes. For instance, consider the following chromosomes and crossover points at positions 2 and 5.

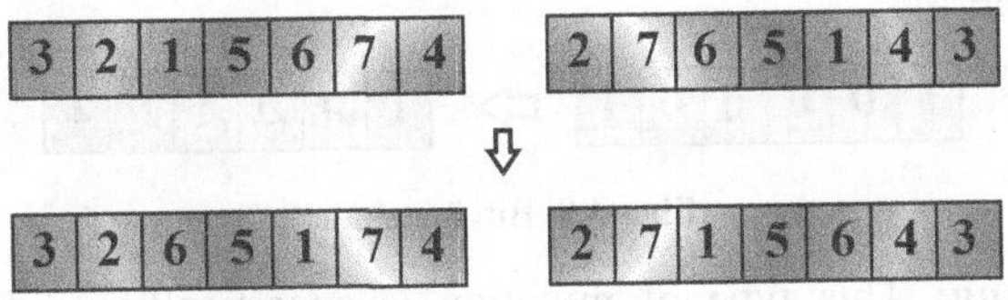

Fig. 4.6 Two point crossover

Here we observe that the crossover regions between the crossover points are interchanged in the children.

***(c)* Tree Crossover:** The tree crossover method is most suitable when tree encoding is employed. One crossover point is chosen at random and parents are divided in that point and parts below crossover point are exchanged to produce new offspring.

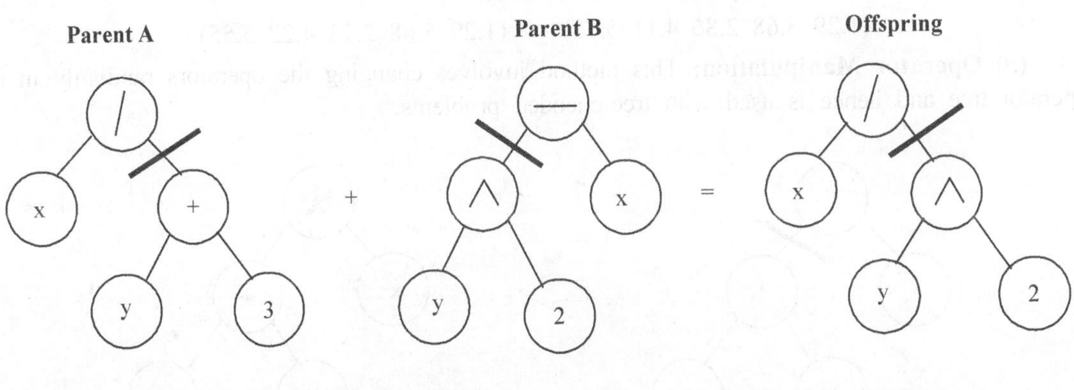

Fig. 4.7 Tree crossover

4.5.2 Mutation

As new individuals are generated, each character is mutated with a given probability. In a binary-coded Genetic Algorithm, mutation may be done by flipping a bit, while in a non-binary-coded GA, mutation involves randomly generating a new character in a specified position. Mutation produces incremental random changes in the offspring generated through crossover. When used by itself without any crossover, mutation is equivalent to a random search consisting of incremental random modification of the existing solution and acceptance if there is improvement. However, when used in the GA, its behavior changes radically. In the GA, mutation serves the crucial role for replacing the gene values lost from the population during the selection process so that they can be tried in a new context, or of providing the gene values that were not present in the initial population.

The type of mutation used as in crossover is dependent on the type of encoding employed. The various types are as follows:

***(a)* Bit Inversion:** This mutation type is employed for a binary encoded problem. Here, a bit is randomly selected and inverted *i.e.*, a bit is changed from 0 to 1 and vice-versa. For instance, consider mutation at allele 4.

Fig. 4.8 Bit inversion

***(b)* Order Changing:** This type of mutation is specifically used in permutation-encoded problems. Here, two random points in the chromosome are chosen and interchanged. For instance,

Fig. 4.9 Order changing

***(c)* Value Manipulation:** Value manipulation refers to selecting random point or points in the chromosome and adding or subtracting a small number from it. Hence, this method is specifically useful for real value encoded problems. For instance,

(1.29 5.68 2.86 4.11 5.55) => (1.29 5.68 2.73 4.22 5.55)

***(d)* Operator Manipulation:** This method involves changing the operators randomly in an operator tree and hence is used with tree-encoded problems.

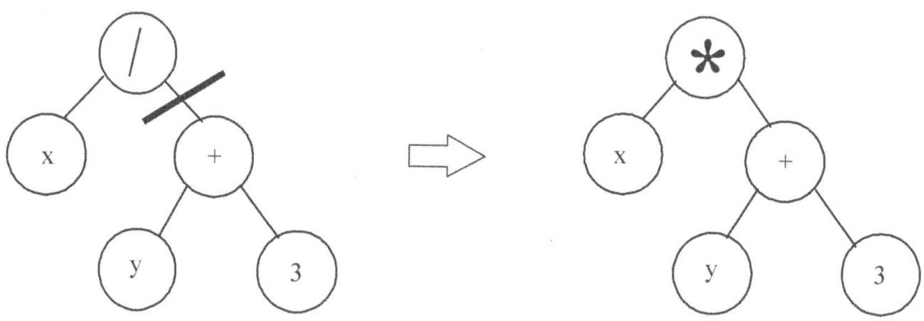

Fig. 4.10 Operator manipulation

Here we observe that the divide operator in the parent is randomly changed to the multiplication operator.

4.6 CLUSTERING

4.6.1 What is Clustering?

Clustering can be considered the most important unsupervised learning problem; so, as every other problem of this kind, deals with finding a structure in a collection of unlabeled data.

Definition of clustering could be **"the process of organizing objects into groups whose members are similar in some way"**.

A *cluster* is therefore a collection of objects which are "similar" between them and are "dissimilar" to the objects belonging to other clusters.

Graphical Example

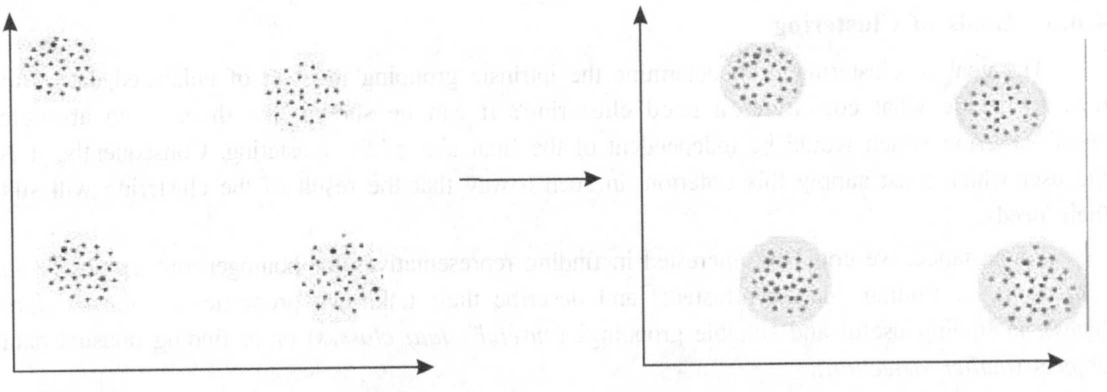

Fig. 4.11 Clustering process-example

In the example, we easily identify the 4 clusters into which the data can be divided; the similarity criterion is distance: two or more objects belong to the same cluster if they are "close" according to a given distance (in this case geometrical distance). This is called **distance-based clustering**.

Another kind of clustering is **conceptual clustering**: two or more objects belong to the same cluster if this one defines a concept common to all that objects. In other words, objects are grouped according to their fit to descriptive concepts, not according to simple similarity measures.

4.6.2 Distance Functions

Given two *p*-dimensional data objects $i = (x_{i1}, x_{i2}, ..., x_{ip})$ and $j = (x_{j1}, x_{j2}, ..., x_{jp})$, the following common distance functions can be defined:

Euclidean Distance Function

$$d(i,j) = \sqrt{|x_{i1} - x_{j1}|^2 + |x_{i2} - x_{j2}|^2 + ... + |x_{ip} - x_{jp}|^2}$$

Manhattan Distance Function

$$d(i,j) = |x_{i1} - x_{j1}| + |x_{i2} - x_{j2}| + ... + |x_{ip} - x_{jp}|$$

When using the Euclidean distance function to compare distances, it is not necessary to calculate the square root because distances are always positive numbers and as such, for two distances, d_1 and d_2, $\sqrt{d_1} > \sqrt{d_2} \Leftrightarrow d_1 > d_2$. If some of an object's attributes are measured along different scales, so when using the Euclidean distance function, attributes with larger scales of measurement may overwhelm attributes measured on a smaller scale. To prevent this problem, the attribute values are often normalized to lie between 0 and 1.

4.6.3 Goals of Clustering

The goal of clustering is to determine the intrinsic grouping in a set of unlabeled data. But how to decide what constitutes a good clustering? It can be shown that there is no absolute "best" criterion which would be independent of the final aim of the clustering. Consequently, it is the user which must supply this criterion, in such a way that the result of the clustering will suit their needs.

For instance, we could be interested in finding representatives for homogeneous groups (*data reduction*), in finding "natural clusters" and describe their unknown properties (*"natural" data types*), in finding useful and suitable groupings (*"useful" data classes*) or in finding unusual data objects (*outlier detection*).

4.6.4 Applications

Clustering algorithms can be applied in many fields, for instance:

- **Marketing:** finding groups of customers with similar behavior given a large database of customer data containing their properties and past buying records;
- **Biology:** classification of plants and animals given their features;
- **Libraries:** book ordering;
- **Insurance:** identifying groups of motor insurance policy holders with a high average claim cost; identifying frauds;
- **City-planning:** identifying groups of houses according to their house type, value and geographical location;
- **Earthquake studies:** clustering observed earthquake epicenters to identify dangerous zones;
- **WWW:** document classification; clustering weblog data to discover groups of similar access patterns.

4.6.5 Types of Clustering Algorithms

There are two types of clustering algorithms: 1. **Nonhierarchical** and 2. **Hierarchical.**

In nonhierarchical clustering, such as the k-means algorithm, the relationship between clusters is undetermined. Hierarchical clustering repeatedly links pairs of clusters until every data object is included in the hierarchy. With both of these approaches, an important issue is how to determine the similarity between two objects, so that clusters can be formed from objects with a high similarity to each other.

4.6.5.1 Nonhierarchical Algorithms

K-means Algorithm

The *k*-means algorithm is one of a group of algorithms called **partitioning methods.** The problem of partitioned clustering can be formally stated as follows: Given n objects in a *d*-dimensional metric space, determine a partition of the objects into *k* groups, or clusters, such that the objects in a cluster are more similar to each other than to objects in different clusters. Recall that a partition divides a set into disjoint parts that together include all members of the set. The value of *k* may or may not be specified and a clustering criterion, typically the **squared-error criterion**, must be adopted.

The solution to this problem is straightforward. Select a clustering criterion, then for each data object select the cluster that optimizes the criterion. The *k*-means algorithm initializes *k* clusters by arbitrarily selecting one object to represent each cluster. Each of the remaining objects is assigned to a cluster and the clustering criterion is used to calculate the cluster mean. These means are used as the new cluster points and each object is reassigned to the cluster that it is most similar to. This continues until there is no longer a change when the clusters are recalculated. The algorithm is shown in Fig. 4.12.

> ***k*-means Algorithm:**
>
> 1. Select *k* clusters arbitrarily.
> 2. Initialize cluster centers with those *k* clusters.
> 3. Do loop
>   (a) Partition by assigning or reassigning all data objects to their closest cluster center.
>   (b) Compute new cluster centers as mean value of the objects in each cluster until no change in cluster center calculation.

Fig. 4.12 *k*-means algorithm

Example

$$P_i = \begin{bmatrix} 0 & 0 \\ 0 & 1 \\ 1 & 1 \\ 1 & 0 \\ 0.5 & 0.5 \\ 5 & 5 \\ 5 & 6 \\ 6 & 6 \\ 6 & 5 \\ 5.5 & 5.5 \end{bmatrix}$$

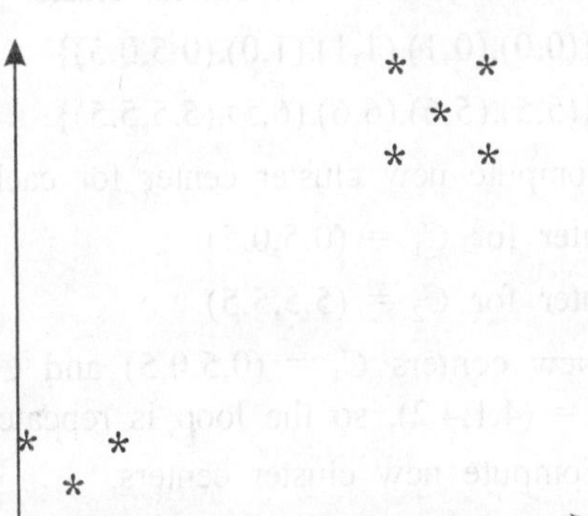

Fig. 4.13 Sample data—*k*-means clustering process

Suppose we are given the data in Fig. 4.13 as input and we choose $k = 2$ and the Manhattan distance function $dis = |x_2 - x_1| + |y_2 - y_1|$. The detailed computation is as follows:

Step 1: Initialize k partitions. An initial partition can be formed by first specifying a set of k seed points. The seed points could be the first k objects or k objects chosen randomly from the input objects. We choose the first two objects as seed points and initialize the clusters as $C_1 = \{(0,0)\}$ and $C_2 = \{(0,1)\}$.

Step 2: Since there is only one point in each cluster, that point is the cluster center.

Step 3a: Calculate the distance between each object and each cluster center, assigning the object to the closest cluster.

For example, for the third object:

$dis(1,3) = |1-0| + |1-0| = 2$ and

$dis(2,3) = |1-0| + |1-1| = 1$,

so this object is assigned to C_2.

The fifth object is equidistant from both clusters, so we arbitrarily assign it to C_1.

After calculating the distance for all points, the clusters contain the following objects:

$C_1 = \{(0,0),(1,0),(0.5,0.5)\}$ and

$C_2 = \{(0,1),(1,1),(5,5),(5,6),(6,6),(6,5),(5.5,5.5)\}$.

Step 3b: Compute new cluster center for each cluster.

New center for $C_1 = (0.5,0.16)$

$(0+1+0.5)/3 = 0.5$

$(0+0+0.5)/3 = 0.16$

New center for $C_2 = (4.1,4.2)$

$(0+1+5+5+6+6+5.5)/7 = 4.1$

$(1+1+5+5+6+6+5.5)/7 = 4.2$.

Step 3a′: New centers $C_1 = (0.5,0.16)$ and $C_2 = (4.1,4.2)$ differ from old centers $C_1=\{(0,0)\}$ and $C_2=\{(0,1)\}$, so the loop is repeated.

Reassign the ten objects to the closest cluster center, resulting in:

$C_1 = \{(0,0),(0,1),(1,1),(1,0),(0.5,0.5)\}$

$C_2 = \{(5,5),(5,6),(6,6),(6,5),(5.5,5.5)\}$.

Step 3b′: Compute new cluster center for each cluster

New center for $C_1 = (0.5,0.5)$

New center for $C_2 = (5.5,5.5)$.

Step 3a″: New centers $C_1 = (0.5,0.5)$ and $C_2 = (5.5,5.5)$ differ from old centers $C_1 = (0.5,0.16)$ and $C_2 = (4.1,4.2)$, so the loop is repeated.

Step 3b″: Compute new cluster centers.

Algorithm is done: Centers are the same as in Step 3b′, so algorithm is finished. Result is same as in 3b′.

4.6.5.2 Hierarchical Clustering

Hierarchical clustering creates hierarchy of clusters on the data set. This hierarchical tree shows levels of clustering with each level having a larger number of smaller clusters.

Hierarchical algorithms can be either agglomerative or divisive, that is top-down or bottom-up. All **agglomerative hierarchical clustering algorithms** begin with each object as a separate group. These groups are successively combined based on similarity until there is only one group remaining or a specified termination condition is satisfied. For n objects, n-1 mergings are done. **Hierarchical algorithms** are rigid in that once a merge has been done, it cannot be undone. Although there are smaller computational costs with this, it can also cause problems if an erroneous merge is done. As such, merge points need to be chosen carefully. Here we describe a simple agglomerative clustering algorithm.

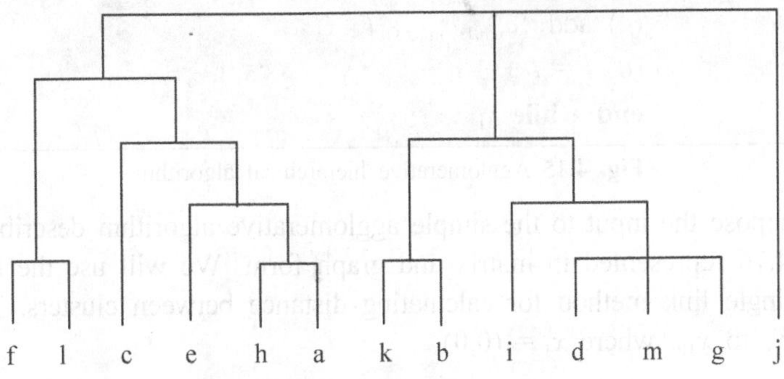

Fig. 4.14 Sample dendogram without clustering process

In the context of hierarchical clustering, the hierarchy graph is called a **dendogram**. Fig. 4.14 shows a sample dendogram that could be produced from a hierarchical clustering algorithm. Unlike with the k-means algorithm, the number of clusters (k) is not specified in hierarchical clustering. After the hierarchy is built, the user can specify the number of clusters required, from 1 to n. The top level of the hierarchy represents one cluster, or k = 1. To examine more clusters, we simply need to traverse down the hierarchy.

Fig. 4.15 shows a simple hierarchical algorithm. The distance function in this algorithm can determine similarity of clusters through many methods, including single link and group-average. **Single link** calculates the distance between two clusters as the shortest distance between any two objects contained in those clusters. **Group-average** first finds the average values for all objects in the group (*i.e.*, cluster) and calculates the distance between clusters as the distance between the average values.

Each object in X is initially used to create a cluster containing a single object. These clusters are successively merged into new clusters, which are added to the set of clusters, C. When a pair of clusters is merged, the original clusters are removed from C. Thus, the number of clusters in C decreases until there is only one cluster remaining, containing all the objects from X. The hierarchy of clusters is implicitly represented in the nested sets of C.

Given:

A set X of objects $\{x_1,\ldots,x_n\}$

A distance function $dis(c_1,c_2)$

1. **for** $i = 1$ to n

   $c_i = \{x_i\}$

   end for

2. $C = \{c_1,\ldots,c_b\}$
3. $l = n+1$
4. **while** C.size > 1 **do**

   (a) $(c_{\min 1}, c_{\min 2})$ = minimum $dis(c_i,c_j)$ for all c_i,c_j in C

   (b) remove $c_{\min 1}$ and $c_{\min 2}$ from C

   (c) add $\{c_{\min 1}, c_{\min 2}\}$ to C

   (d) $l = l + 1$

   end while

Fig. 4.15 Agglomerative hierarchical algorithm

Example: Suppose the input to the simple agglomerative algorithm described above is the set X, shown in Fig. 4.16 represented in matrix and graph form. We will use the Manhattan distance function and the single link method for calculating distance between clusters. The set X contains $n = 10$ elements, x_1 to x_{10}, where $x_1 = (0,0)$.

$$X = \begin{bmatrix} 0 & 0 \\ 1 & 1 \\ 3 & 1 \\ 2 & 4 \\ 6 & 3 \\ 6 & 6 \\ 5 & 2 \\ 3 & 5 \\ 0 & 2 \\ 2 & 1 \end{bmatrix}$$

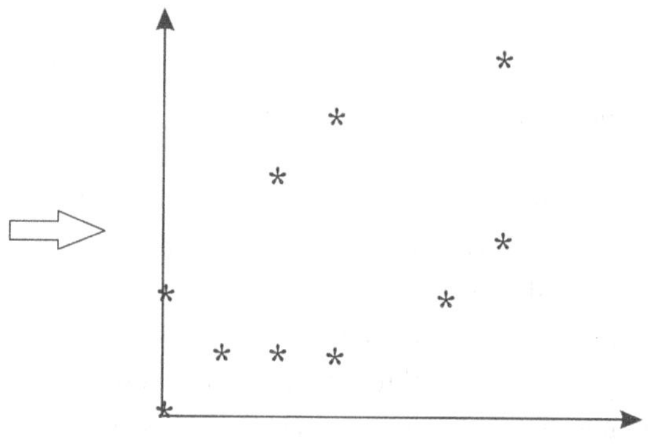

Fig. 4.16 Sample data

Step 1: Initially, each element x_i of X is placed in a cluster c_i, where c_i is a member of the set of clusters C.

$C = \{\{x_1\},\{x_2\},\{x_3\}, \{x_4\},\{x_5\},\{x_6\},\{x_7\}, \{x_8\},\{x_9\},\{x_{10}\}\}$

Step 2: Set $l = 11$.

Step 3: (First iteration of while loop) C.size = 10

✧ The minimum single link distance between two clusters is 1. This occurs in two places, between c_2 and c_{10} and between c_3 and c_{10}.

Depending on how our minimum function works we can choose either pair of clusters. Arbitrarily we choose the first.

$$(c_{min1}, c_{min2}) = (c_2, c_{10})$$

✧ Since $l = 10$, $c_{11} = c_2 \cup c_{10} = \{\{x_2\},\{x_{10}\}\}$

✧ Remove c_2 and c_{10} from C.

✧ Add c_{11} to C.

$$C = \{\{x_1\},\{x_3\}, \{x_4\},\{x_5\},\{x_6\},\{x_7\}, \{x_8\},\{x_9\},\{\{x_2\}, \{x_{10}\}\}\}$$

✧ Set $l = l + 1 = 12$.

Step 3: (Second iteration) C.size = 9

✧ The minimum single link distance between two clusters is 1. This occurs between, between c_3 and c_{11} because the distance between x_3 and x_{10} is 1, where x_{10} is in c_{11}.

$$(c_{min1}, c_{min2}) = (c_3, c_{11})$$

✧ $c_{12} = c_3 \cup c_{11} = \{\{\{x_2\},\{x_{10}\}\},\{x_3\}\}$

✧ Remove c_3 and c_{11} from C.

✧ Add c_{12} to C.

$$C = \{\{x_1\}, \{x_4\},\{x_5\},\{x_6\},\{x_7\}, \{x_8\},\{x_9\},\{\{\{x_2\}, \{x_{10}\}\}, \{x_3\}\}\}$$

✧ Set $l = 13$.

Step 3: (Third iteration) C.size = 8

✧ $(c_{min1}, c_{min2}) = (c_1, c_{12})$

✧ $C = \{\{x_4\},\{x_5\},\{x_6\},\{x_7\}, \{x_8\},\{x_9\},\{\{\{\{x_2\}, \{x_{10}\}\}, \{x_3\}\},\{x_1\}\}\}$

Step 3: (Fourth iteration) C.size = 7

✧ $(c_{min1}, c_{min2}) = (c_4, c_8)$

✧ $C = \{\{x_5\},\{x_6\},\{x_7\}, \{x_9\},\{\{\{\{x_2\}, \{x_{10}\}\}, \{x_3\}\},\{x_1\}\},\{\{x_4\},\{x_8\}\}\}$

Step 3: (Fifth iteration) C.size = 6

✧ $(c_{min1}, c_{min2}) = (c_5, c_7)$

✧ $C = \{\{x_6\}, \{x_9\},\{\{\{\{x_2\}, \{x_{10}\}\}, \{x_3\}\},\{x_1\}\},\{\{x_4\},\{x_8\}\}, \{\{x_5\},\{x_7\}\}\}$

Step 3: (Sixth iteration) C.size = 5

✧ $(c_{min1}, c_{min2}) = (c_9, c_{13})$

✧ $C = \{\{x_6\}, \{\{x_4\},\{x_8\}\}, \{\{x_5\},\{x_7\}\},\{\{\{\{\{x_2\}, \{x_{10}\}\}, \{x_3\}\},\{x_1\}\},\{x_9\}\}\}$

Step 3: (Seventh iteration) C.size = 4

✧ $(c_{min1}, c_{min2}) = (c_6, c_{15})$

✧ $C = \{\{\{x_4\},\{x_8\}\}, \{\{\{\{\{x_2\}, \{x_{10}\}\}, \{x_3\}\},\{x_1\}\},\{x_9\}\},\{\{x_6\}, \{\{x_5\},\{x_7\}\}\}\}$

Step 3: (Eighth iteration) C.size = 3

✧ $(c_{min1}, c_{min2}) = (c_{14}, c_{16})$

✧ $C = \{\ \{\{x_6\},\ \{\{x_5\},\{x_7\}\}\},\ \{\{\{x_4\},\{x_8\}\},\ \{\{\{\{\{x_2\},\ \{x_{10}\}\},\ \{x_3\}\},\{x_1\}\},\{x_9\}\}\}\}$

Step 3: (Ninth iteration) *C*.size = 2

✧ $(c_{min1}, c_{min2}) = (c_{17}, c_{18})$

✧ $C = \{\{\{\{x_4\},\{x_8\}\},\ \{\{\{\{\{x_2\},\ \{x_{10}\}\},\ \{x_3\}\},\{x_1\}\},\{x_9\}\}\},\ \{\{x_6\},\ \{\{x_5\},\{x_7\}\}\}\}$

Step 3: (Tenth iteration) *C*.size = 1. Algorithm done.

The cluster created from this algorithm can be seen in Fig. 4.17. The corresponding dendogram formed from the hierarchy in *C* is shown in Fig. 4.18. The points which appeared most closely together on the graph of input data in Fig. 4.16 are grouped together more closely in the hierarchy.

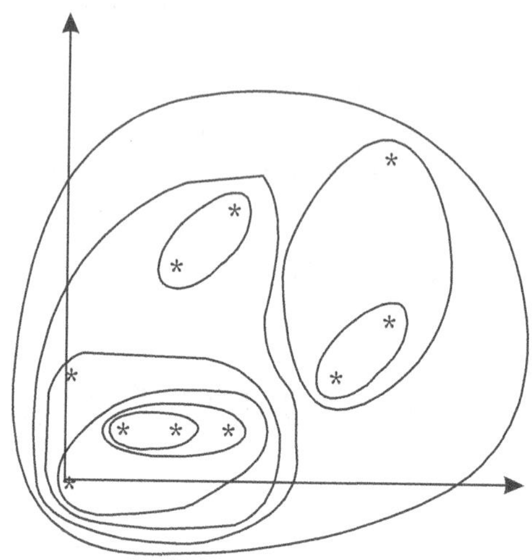

Fig. 4.17 Graph with clusters

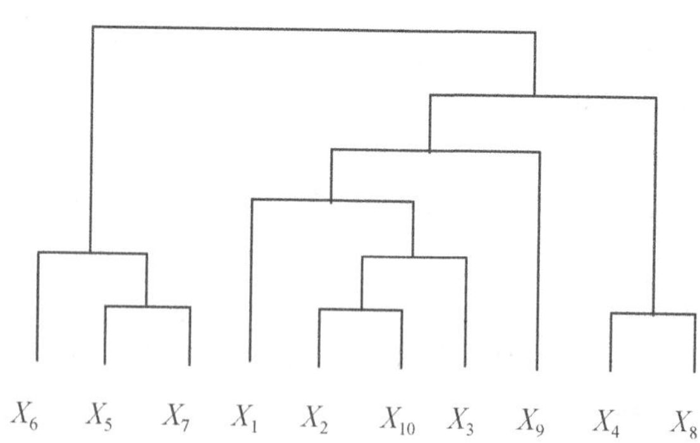

Fig. 4.18 Sample dendogram after clustering

4.6.5.3 Other Hierarchical Clustering Methods

1. Single Link Method

- *Similarity:* Join the most similar pair of objects that are not yet in the same cluster. Distance between 2 clusters is the distance between the closest pair of points, each of which is in one of the two clusters.
- *Type of clusters:* Long straggly clusters, chains, ellipsoidal.
- *Time:* Usually O(N**2) though can range from O(N log N) to O(N**5).
- *Space:* O(N).
- *Advantages:* Theoretical properties, efficient implementations, widely used. No cluster centroid or representative required, so no need arises to recalculate the similarity matrix.
- *Disadvantages:* Unsuitable for isolating spherical or poorly separated clusters.

SLINK Algorithms

- Array record cluster pointer and distance information
- Process input documents one by one. For each:
- Compute and store a row of the distance matrix
- Find nearest other point, using the matrix
- Relabel clusters, as needed

MST Algorithms

- MST has all info needed to generate single link hierarchy in O(N**2) operations, or the single link hierarchy can be built at the same time as MST.
- Prim-Dijkstra algorithm operates as follows:
- Place an arbitrary document in the MST and connect its NN (Nearest Neighbor) to it, to create an initial MST fragment.
- Find the document not in the MST that is closest to any point in the MST, and add it to the current MST fragment.
- If a document remains that is not in the MST fragment, repeat the previous step.

2. Complete Link Method

- *Similarity*: Join least similar pair between each of two clusters
- *Type of clusters*: All entries in a cluster are linked to one another within some minimum similarity, so have small, tightly bound clusters.
- *Time*: Voorhees alg. worst case is O(N**3) but sparse matrices require much less
- *Space*: Voorhees alg. worst case is O(N**2) but sparse matrices require much less
- *Advantages*: Good results from (Voorhees) comparative studies.
- *Disadvantages*: Difficult to apply to large data sets since most efficient algorithm is general Hierarchical agglomerative clustering method (HACM) using stored data or stored matrix approach.

Voorhees Algorithm

- ✧ Variation on the sorted matrix HACM approach
- ✧ Based on fact: if sims between all pairs of docs are processed in descending order, two clusters of size m_i and m_j can be merged as soon as the $m_i \times m_j$ th similarity of documents in those clusters is reached.
- ✧ Requires sorted list of doc-doc similarities
- ✧ Requires way to count no. of sims seen between any 2 active clusters

3. Group Average Link Method

- ✧ *Similarity*: Use the average value of the pairwise links within a cluster, based upon all objects in the cluster. Save space and time if use inner product of 2 (appropriately weighted) vectors — see Voorhees alg. below.
- ✧ *Type of clusters*: Intermediate in tightness between single link and complete link
- ✧ *Time*: O(N**2)
- ✧ *Space*: O(N)
- ✧ *Advantages*: Ranked well in evaluation studies
- ✧ *Disadvantages*: Expensive for large collections

Algorithm

- ✧ Sim between cluster centroid and any doc = mean sim between the doc and all docs in the cluster.
- ✧ Hence, can use centroids only to compute cluster-cluster sim, in O(N) space

Ward's Method (minimum variance method)

- ✧ *Similarity*: Join the cluster pair whose merger minimizes the increase in the total within-group error sum of squares, based on Euclidean distance between centroids
- ✧ *Type of clusters*: Homogeneous clusters in a symmetric hierarchy; cluster centroid nicely characterized by its center of gravity
- ✧ *Time*: O(N**2)
- ✧ *Space*: O(N) — carries out agglomerations in restricted spatial regions
- ✧ *Advantages*: Good at recovering cluster structure, yields unique and exact hierarchy
- ✧ *Disdvantages*: Sensitive to outliers, poor at recovering elongated clusters

RNN:

We can apply a reciprocal nearest neighbor (RNN) algorithm, since for any point or cluster there exists a chain of nearest neighbors (NNs) that ends with a pair that are each others' NN.

Algorithm - Single Cluster:

1. Select an arbitrary doc
2. Follow the NN chain from it till an RNN pair is found.

3. Merge the 2 points in that pair, replacing them with a single new point.
4. If there is only one point, stop. Otherwise, if there is a point in the NN chain preceding the merged points, return to step 2 else to step 1.

4. Centroid and Median methods

- *Similarity*: At each stage join the pair of clusters with the most similar centroids.
- *Type of clusters*: Cluster is represented by the coordinates of the group centroid or median.
- *Disadvantages*: Newly formed clusters may differ overly much from constituent points, meaning that updates may cause large changes throughout the cluster hierarchy.

General algorithm for HACM

All hierarchical agglomerative clustering methods (HACMs) can be described by the following general algorithm.

Algorithm

1. Identify the 2 closest points and combine them into a cluster
2. Identify and combine the next 2 closest points (treating existing clusters as points too)
3. If more than one cluster remains, return to step 1.

How to apply general algorithm?

Lance and Williams proposed the Lance-Williams dissimilarity update formula, to calculate dissimilarities between a new cluster and existing points, based on the dissimilarities prior to forming the new cluster. This formula has 3 parameters, and each HACM can be characterized by its own set of Lance-Williams parameters. Then, the algorithm above can be applied, using the appropriate Lance-Williams dissimilarities.

Implementations of the general algorithm

- *Stored matrix* approach: Use matrix, and then apply Lance-Williams to recalculate dissimilarities between cluster centers. Storage is therefore O(N**2) and time is at least O(N**2), but will be O(N**3) if matrix is scanned linearly.
- *Stored data* approach: O(N) space for data but recompute pairwise dissimilarities so need O(N**3) time
- *Sorted matrix* approach: O(N**2) to calculate dissimilarity matrix, O(N**2 log N**2) to sort it, O(N**2) to construct hierarchy, but one need not store the data set, and the matrix can be processed linearly, which reduces disk accesses.

4.7 ONLINE ANALYTIC PROCESSING (OLAP)

The term *On-Line Analytic Processing - OLAP* (or *Fast Analysis of Shared Multidimensional Information - FASMI*) refers to technology that allows users of multidimensional databases to generate on-line descriptive or comparative summaries ("views") of data and other analytic queries. Note that despite its name, analyses referred to as *OLAP* do not need to be performed truly "on-line" (or in real-time); the term applies to analyses of multidimensional databases (that may, obviously, contain dynamically updated information) through efficient "multidimensional" queries that reference various types of data. *OLAP* facilities can be integrated into corporate (enterprise-wide) database systems and they allow analysts and managers to monitor the performance of the business (*e.g.*, such as various aspects of the manufacturing process or numbers and types of completed transactions at different locations) or the market. The final result of *OLAP* techniques can be very simple (*e.g.*, frequency tables, descriptive statistics, simple cross-tabulations) or more complex (*e.g.*, they may involve seasonal adjustments, removal of outliers, and other forms of cleaning the data). More information about OLAP is discussed in Chapter 6.

4.8 ASSOCIATION RULES

Association rule mining finds interesting associations and/or correlation relationships among large set of data items. Association rules show attributes value conditions that occur frequently together in a given dataset. A typical and widely-used example of association rule mining is Market Basket Analysis.

Discovery of association rules are showing attribute-value conditions that occur frequently together in a given set of data. Market Basket Analysis is a modeling technique based on the theory that if you buy a certain group of items then you are more (or less) likely to buy another group of items. The set of items a customer buys is referred to as an item set, and market basket analysis seeks to find relationships between purchases.

Typically the relationship will be in the form of a rule:

IF {bread} THEN {butter}.

This above condition extracts the hidden information *i.e.*, if a customer used to buy bread, he will also buy butter as side dish.

The minimum percentage of instances in the database that contain all items listed in a given association rule.

There are two types of Association rule levels.

Support Level

Confidence Level

4.8.1 Rules for Support Level

The minimum percentage of instances in the database that contain all items listed in a given association rule.

Support of an item set

Let *T* be the set of all transactions under consideration, *e.g.*, let T be the set of all "baskets" or "carts" of products bought by the customers from a supermarket – say on a given day. The support of an item set *S* is the percentage of those transactions in *T* which contain *S*. In the supermarket example this is the number of "baskets" that contain a given set S of products, for example S = {bread, butter, milk}. If U is the set of all transactions that contain all items in S, then

$$\text{Support}(S) = (|U|/|T|) * 100\%$$

where $|U|$ and $|T|$ are the number of elements in U and T, respectively. For example, if a customer buys the set X = {milk, bread, apples, banana, sausages, cheese, onions, potatoes} then S is obviously a subset of X, and hence S is in U. If there are 318 customers and 242 of them buy such a set U or a similar one that contains S, then support (S) = (242/318) = 76.1%.

4.8.2 Rules for Confidence Level

"If A then B", rule confidence is the conditional probability that B is true when A is known to be true.

Confidence of an association rule

To evaluate association rules, the confidence of a rule R = "A and B -> C" is the support of the set of all items that appear in the rule divided by the support of the antecedent of the rule, *i.e.*,

$$\text{Confidence } (R) = (\text{support } (\{A, B, C\})/\text{support } (\{A, B\})) * 100\%$$

More intuitively, the confidence of a rule is the number of cases in which the rule is correct relative to the number of cases in which it is applicable. For example, let R = "butter and bread -> *milk*". If a customer buys butter and bread, then the rule is applicable and it says that he/she can be expected to buy milk. If he/she does not buy sugar or does not buy bread or buys neither, than the rule is not applicable and thus (obviously) does not say anything about this customer.

4.8.3 APRIORI Algorithm

The first algorithm to generate all frequent sets and confident association rules was the AIS algorithm by Agrawal *et al.*, which was given together with the introduction of this mining problem. Shortly after that, the algorithm was improved and renamed Apriori by Agrawal *et al.* by exploiting the monotonic property of the frequency of item sets and the confidence of association rules

Frequent item set mining problem

A *transactional database* consists of sequence of transaction: $T = (t1,\ldots,tn)$. A transaction is a set of items (t, ∈, I). Transactions are often called baskets, referring to the primary application domain (*i.e.*, market-basket analysis). A set of items is often called the *item set* by the data mining community. The (*absolute*) *support* or the *occurrence* of X (denoted by Supp(X) is the number of transactions that are supersets of X (*i.e.*, that *contain* X). The *relative support* is the absolute support divided by the number of transactions (*i.e.*, n). An item set is *frequent* if its support is greater or equal to a threshold value.

Association rule mining problem

This program is also capable of mining association rules. An association rule is like an implication: X -> Y means that if item set X occurs in a transaction, then item set Y also occurs with high probability. This probability is given by the *confidence* of the rule. It is like an approximation of *p(Y|X)*, it is the number of transactions that contain both X and Y divided by the number of transaction that contain *X*, thus conf(*X*–>*Y*) = Supp(*XUY*)/Supp(*X*). An association rule is *valid* if its confidence and support are greater than or equal to corresponding threshold values.

In the frequent itemset mining problem a transaction database and a relative support threshold (traditionally denoted by *min_supp*) is given and we have to find all frequent itemsets.

Apriori steps are as follows:

Counts item occurrences to determine the frequent item sets.

Candidates are generated.

Count the support of item sets pruning process ensures candidate sizes are already known to be frequent item sets.

Use the frequent item sets to generate the desired rules.

Algorithm

```
Input
        I               // Itemsets
        D               // Database of transactions
        S               // Support
Output
        L               // Large Itemsets
Apriori Algorithm
        k = 0           // k is used as the scan number
        L = 0
        Ci = I          // Initial candidates are set to be the items
        Ck
        Repeat
                        k = k + 1
                        Lk = 0
                        For each Ii ∈ Ck do
                                ci = 0 // initial counts for each itset are 0
                        for each tj ∈ D do
                                for each Ii ∈ Ck do
                                        if Ii ∈ tj then
                                                ci = ci +1
                        for each Ii ∈ Ck do
                                if ci >= (s x |D|) do
                                        Lk = Lk U Ii
                        L = L U Lk
```

C_k+1 = Apriori_Gen(L_k)

Until C_k+1 =0

Input

$L_i - 1$ // Large Itemsets of size i–1

Output

C_i // Candidate of size i

Apriori-gen algorithm

C_i = 0

For each I ∈ L_{i-1} do

For each J ≠ I ∈ L_{i-1} do

If i-2 of the elements in I and J are equal then

$C_k = C_k$ U (I U J)

AR Gen algorithm

Input

D // Database of transactions

I // Items

L // Large Itemsets

S // Support

œ // Confidence

Output

R // Association rules satisfying s and œ

AR Gen Algorithm

R=0

For each I ∈ L do

For each x C I such that x ≠0 do

If support(I)/support(x) >= œ then

R=RU(x = > (1 – X))

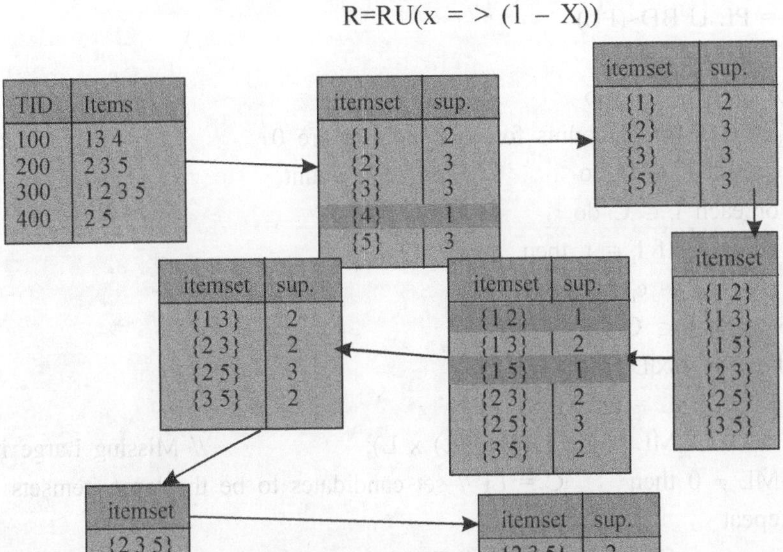

Fig. 4.19 *Apriori* example

Rules from example

Support(2 3) = 2/4*100 = 50
Support(2 3 5) = 2/4*100 = 50
Confidence(2 3→5) = Support(2 3 5)/support(2 3) = 50/50*100=100%
2 3 → 5 (Support 50%, Confidence 100%)

4.8.4 Sampling Algorithm

Here a sample is drawn from the database such that it is memory resident. Then any one algorithm is used to find the large item sets for the sample. In an item set is large in a sample; it is viewed to be potentially large in the entire database.

Advantages

(1) Facilitates efficient counting of item sets in large databases.

(2) Original sampling algorithm reduces the number of database scans to one or two.

```
Input:
        I           // Item set
        D           // Database of transactions
        S           // Support
Output:
        L           // Large item set
Sampling algorithm:
        Ds = Sample drawn from Di
        PL = Apriori(I,Ds,smalls)
        C = PL U BD~(PL)
        L = 0
        For each Ii ∈ C do
         ci = 0 // Initial counts for each itemset are 0
        For each tj ∈ D do          // First scan count
         For each Ii ∈ C do
                   If Ii ∈ tj then
                     ci = ci + 1
        For each Ii ∈ C do
         If ci >= (sx|D|) do
                   L = L U Ii
                   ML = (x| x BD~(PL) x L);          // Missing Large itemsets
        If ML ≠ 0 then      C = Li // set candidates to be the large itemsets
         Repeat
                   C = C U BD~© // Expand candidate sets using negative border
          Until no new itemsets are added to C;
```

For each $I_i \in C$ do

$c_i = 0$ // Initial counts for each itemset are 0

For each $t_j \in D$ do // Second scan count

For each $I_i \in C$ do

If $I_i \in t_j$ then

$c_i = c_i + 1$

If $c_i \geqslant (sx|D|$ then $L = L \cup I_i$

4.8.5 Partitioning Algorithm

Here the database D is divided into 'P' partitions $D^1, D^2, \ldots, D^n$.

Advantages

(1) Algorithm is more efficient as it has the advantages of large itemset property wherein a large itemsets must be large in at least one of the partitions.

(2) These algorithms adapt better to binted main memory.

(3) It is easier to perform incremental generation of association rules by heating the current style of database as one partition and treating the new entries as a second partitions.

Input

I // Item set

$D = (D^1, D^2, \ldots. D^p)$ // Database of transactions divided into partition

S // Support

Output

L // Large Itemset

Partitioning Algorithm

C=0

For I = 1 to p do // Find large itemsets in each partition

L_i = *Apriori*(I, D^i, s)

$C = CUL^i$

L = 0

For each $I_i \in C$ do

$c_i=0$ // Initial counts for each item set are 0.

For each $t_j \in D$ do // count candidates during second scan

For each $I_i \in C$ do

$I_i \in t_j$ then

$c_i = c_i + 1$

For each $I_i \in C$ do

If $c_i \geqslant (sx|D|)$ then

$L = L \cup I_i$

4.9 EMERGING TRENDS IN DATA MINING

4.9.1 Web Mining

Web mining is mining of data related to the World Wide Web. This may be the data actually present in Web pages or data related to Web activity. Web data can be classified into the following classes.

Content of actual web pages

Intra page structure includes the HTML or XML code for the page

Inter page structure is the actual linkage structure between web

Usage data that describe how Web pages are accessed by visitors

User profiles include demographic and registration information obtained about users.

Web mining taxonomy

The following are the classification of web mining:

Web content mining

Web page content mining

Search result mining

Web structure mining

Web usage mining

General access pattern tracking

Customized usage tracking.

4.9.2 Spatial Mining

Spatial data are data that a spatial or location component. Spatial data can be viewed as data about objects that themselves are located in physical space. Spatial data are required for many current information technology systems. Geographic information systems are used to store information related to Geographic locations on the surface of the Earth. This includes applications to whether, community infrastructure needs, disaster management, and hazardous waste. Data mining activities include prediction of environmental catastrophes. Biomedical application including medical imaging and illness diagnosis also require spatial system.

Spatial Mining or Spatial data mining or knowledge discovery in spatial databases, is data mining as applied to spatial databases or spatial data. Applications for spatial data mining are GIS system, geology, environment science, resource management, agriculture, medicine and robotics.

4.9.3 Temporal Mining

The data that are stored reflect data at a single point in time, called a snapshot database. Data are maintained for multiple time points, not just one time point is called temporal database. Each tuple contains the information that is current from the date stored with that tuple to the date stored with the next tuple in temporal order.

4.10 DATA MINING RESEARCH PROJECTS

1. Data Mining in the Insurance Industry
2. Increasing Wagering Turnover Through Data Mining
3. The Transition from Data Warehousing to Data Mining
4. Rule Extraction from Trained Neural Networks
5. Neural Networks for Market Basket Analysis
6. Data Mining for Customer Relationship Management
7. Web Usage Mining using Neural Networks
8. Data Visualization Techniques and their Role in Data Mining
9. Evolutionary Rule Generation for Credit Scoring
10. Improved Decision Trees for Data Mining
11. Data Mining in the Pharmaceutical Industry
12. Data Mining the Malaria Genome
13. Neural Network Modeling of Water-Related Gastroenteritis Outbreaks
14. Data Mining with Self Generating Neural Networks
15. Development of Intelligent OLAP Tools
16. Mining Stock Market Data
17. Data Mining by Structure Adapting Neural Networks
18. Rule Discovery with Neural Networks in Different Concept Levels
19. Cash Flow Forecasting using Neural Networks
20. Neural Networks for Market Response Modeling
21. Advertising Effectiveness Modeling
22. Temporal Effects in Direct Marketing Response

EXERCISE

1. What is OLAP? Explain the various tools available for OLAP.
2. Write short notes on (*i*) *Apriori* algorithm, (*ii*) ID3 algorithm.
3. Describe association rule mining and decision trees.
4. What is clustering? Explain.
5. Write in detail about the use of artificial neural network and genetic algorithm for data mining.
6. What is market-basket analysis? Explain with an example.
7. Write an essay on emerging trends in data mining.
8. What is genetic algorithm? Explain.

CHAPTER 5

REAL TIME APPLICATIONS AND FUTURE SCOPE

5.1 APPLICATIONS OF DATA MINING

As on this day, there is not a single field where data mining is not applied. Starting from marketing down to the medical field, data mining tools and techniques have found a niche. They have become the "Hobson's choice" in a number of industrial applications including,

- Ad revenue forecasting
- Churn (turnover) management
- Claims processing
- Credit risk analysis
- Cross-marketing
- Customer profiling
- Customer retention
- Electronic commerce
- Exception reports
- Food-service menu analysis
- Fraud detection
- Government policy setting
- Hiring profiles
- Market basket analysis
- Medical management
- Member enrollment
- New product development
- Pharmaceutical research
- Process control
- Quality control
- Shelf management/store management
- Student recruitment and retention
- Targeted marketing
- Warranty analysis and many more.

The 2003-IBM grading of industries which use data mining are as follows in Table 5.1.

TABLE 5.1 ***Industrial Applications of Data Mining***

Banking	13%
Bioinformatics/Biotechnology	10%
Direct Marketing/Fundraising	10%
eCommerce/Web	5%
Entertainment/News	1%
Fraud Detection	9%
Insurance	8%
Investment/Stocks	3%
Manufacturing	2%
Medical/Pharmacy	6%
Retail	6%
Scientific Data	9%
Security	2%
Supply Chain Analysis	1%
Telecommunications	8%
Travel	2%
Others	4%
None	1%

Industries/fields where data mining is currently applied are as follows:

5.1.1 Data Mining in the Banking Sector

Worldwide, banking sector is ahead of many other industries in using mining techniques for their vast customer database. Although banks have employed statistical analysis tools with some success for several years, previously unseen patterns of customer behavior are now coming into clear focus with the aid of new data mining tools. These statistical tools and even the OLAP find out the answers, but more advanced data mining tools provide insight to the answer.

Some of the applications of data mining in this industry are;

(*i*) Predict customer reaction to the change of interest rates

(*ii*) Identify customers who will be most receptive to new product offers

(*iii*) Identify "loyal" customers

(*iv*) Pin point which clients are at the highest risk for defaulting on a loan

(*v*) Find out persons or groups who will opt for each type of loan in the following year

(*vi*) Detect fraudulent activities in credit card transactions (*vii*) Predict clients who are likely to change their credit card affiliation in the next quarter

(*viii*) Determine customer preference of the different modes of transaction namely through teller or through credit cards, etc.

5.1.2 Data Mining in Bio-Informatics and Biotechnology

Bio-informatics is a rapidly developing research area that has its roots both in biology and information technology.

Various applications of data mining techniques in this field are:

(*i*) prediction of structures of various proteins

(*ii*) determining the intricate structures of several drugs

(*iii*) mapping of DNA structure with base to base accuracy

5.1.3 Data Mining in Direct Marketing and Fund Raising

Marketing is the first field to use data mining tools for its profit.

The many ways in which mining techniques help in direct marketing are;

(*i*) *Differential market basket analysis* helps to decide the location and promotion of goods inside a store and to compare results between different stores, between customers in different demographic groups, between different days of the week, different seasons of the year, etc. to increase company sales.

(*ii*) A predictive market basket analysis can be used to identify sets of item purchases (or events) that generally occur in sequence — something of interest to direct marketers, criminologists and many others.

Techniques followed in data harvesting also help in fund raising (*e.g.*, voluntary organizations, election fund raising, etc.) by;

(*i*) Capturing unlimited data on various donors, volunteers, prospects, agencies and members of different charitable trusts, and access them from one centralized database. Using powerful search options, relationship management and data mining tools, these data are managed and used to build and improve long-term relationships with them.

(*ii*) Setting up multiple funds and default designations based on various criteria such as campaign, region or membership type to honor the donors' wishes.

(*iii*) Defining award classes, assigning requirements and allowing the system to refer the data to automatically generate awards as a recognition of exceptional donor efforts. Communication tools such as the Mass E-Mail Manager make it easy to stay in touch with the constituents.

(*iv*) Providing a flexible communication and campaign management structure from a single appeal through multiple campaigns.

5.1.4 Data Mining in Fraud Detection

Data dredging has found wide and useful application in various fraud detection processes like

(1) Credit card fraud detection using a combined parallel approach

(2) Fraud detection in the voters list using neural networks in combination with symbolic and analog data mining.

(3) Fraud detection in passport applications by designing a specific online learning diagnostic system.

(4) Rule and analog based detection of false medical claims and so on.

5.1.5 Data Mining in Managing Scientific Data

Data Mining is a concept that is taking off in the commercial sector as a means of finding useful information out of gigabytes of scientific data. Gone are those days when scientists have to search through reams of printouts and rooms full of tapes to find the gems that make up scientific discovery.

Few examples of data mining in the scientific environment are:

(1) **Studies on global climatic changes:** This is a *hot* research area and is primarily a verification driven mining exercise. Climate data has been collected for many centuries and is being extended into the more distant past, through such activities as analysis of ice core samples from the Antarctic and, at the same time, a number of different predictive models have been proposed for future climatic conditions. This is an example of Temporal mining as it uses a temporal database maintained for multiple time points.

(2) **Studies on geophysical databases at the University of Helsinki:** It has published a scientific analysis of data on farming and the environment. As a result it has optimized crop yields, while minimizing the resources supplied. To minimize the resources, it identified the factors affecting the crop yield, like chemical fertilizers and additives (phosphate), the moisture content and the type of the soil. This is an example of what known as the spatial mining.

5.1.6 Data Mining in the Insurance Sector

Insurance companies can benefit from modern data mining methodologies, which help companies to reduce costs, increase profits, retain current customers, acquire new customers, and develop new products.

This can be done through:

(1) evaluating the risk of the assets being insured taking into account the characteristics of the asset as well as the owner of the asset.

(2) Formulating Statistical Modeling of Insurance Risks

(3) Using the Joint Poisson/Log-Normal Model of mining to optimize insurance policies

(4) And finally finding the actuarial Credibility of the risk groups among insurers

5.1.7 Data Mining in Telecommunication

As on this date, every activity in telecommunication has used data mining technique.

(1) Analysis of telecom service purchases

(2) Prediction of telephone calling patterns

(3) Management of resources and network traffic

(4) Automation of network management and maintenance using artificial intelligence to diagnose and repair network transmission problems, etc.

5.1.8 Data Mining in Medicine and Pharmacy

Widespread use of medical information systems and explosive growth of medical databases require traditional manual data analysis to be coupled with methods for efficient computer-assisted analysis. Here we present some of the medical and pharmaceutical uses of Data Mining techniques for the analysis of medical databases.

- ✧ Prediction of occurrence of disease and/or complications
- ✧ Therapy of choice for individual cancers
- ✧ Choice of antibiotics for individual infections
- ✧ Choice of a particular technique (of anastamosis, sutures, suture materials etc.) in a given surgical procedures
- ✧ Stocking the most frequently prescribed drugs

And many more...

5.1.9 Data Mining in the Retail Industries

Data mining techniques have gone glove in hand in CRM (Customer Relationship Marketing) by developing models for

- ✧ predicting the propensity of customers to buy
- ✧ assessing risk in each transaction
- ✧ knowing the geographical location and distribution of customers
- ✧ analyzing customer loyalty in credit based transactions
- ✧ Assessing the competitive threat in a locality.

5.1.10 Data Mining in E-Commerce and the World Wide Web

Sophisticated or not, various forms of data-mining development are being undertaken by companies looking to make sense of the raw data that has been mounting relentlessly in the recent years. E-commerce is the newest and hottest to use data mining techniques. A recent article in the *Engineering News-Record* noted that e-commerce has empowered companies to collect vast amounts of data on customers—everything from the number of Web surfers in a home to the value of the cars in their garage. This was possible, the article says, with the use of data mining techniques.

Few of the ways in which data mining tools find its use in e-commerce are:

(1) By formulating market tactics in business operations.

(2) By automating business interactions with customers, so that customers can transact with all the players in supply chain.

(3) By developing common market place services using a shared external ICT infrastructure to manage suppliers and logistics and implement electronic match making mechanisms. This is widely used in today's web world.

Determining the size of the world wide web is extremely difficult. In 1999 it was estimated to contain are 350 billion pages with a growth rate of 1 million page/day. Considering the world wide web to be the largest database collection, web mining can be done in above ways.

5.1.11 Data Mining in Stock Market and Investment

The rapid evolution of computer technology in the last few decades has provided investment professionals (and amateurs) with the capability to access and analyze tremendous amounts of financial data. Data archeology churns the ocean of stock market to obtain the cream of information in ways like,

(*i*) Helping the stock market researchers to predict future stock price movement.

(*ii*) Data mining of the past prices and related variables help to discover stock market anomalies like, the hawala scandal.

5.1.12 Data Mining in Supply Chain Analysis

Supply chain analysis is nothing but the analysis of the various data regarding the transactions between the supplier and the purchaser and the use of this analysis to the advantage of either of them or even both of them.

Data mining techniques have found wide application in supply chain analysis. It is of use to the supplier in the following ways:

(*i*) It analyses the process data to manage buyer rating.

(*ii*) It mines payment data to advantageously update pricing policies

(*iii*) Demand analysis and forecasting helps the supplier to determine the optimum levels of stocks and spare parts.

Coming to the purchaser side in supply chain analysis, data mining techniques help them by:

(*i*) Knowing vendor rating to choose the beneficial supplier.

(*ii*) Analyzing fulfillment data to manage volume purchase contracts.

5.2 FUTURE SCOPE

The era of DBMS began using relational data model and SQL. At present data mining is little there than a set of tools to uncover hidden information from a database. While these are many tools to and this present, there is no all encompassing model or approach. Over the next few years, not only will there be more efficient algorithms with better interface techniques, but also steps will be taken. To develop an all-encompassing model for data mining. While it may not look like the relational model, it probably will include similar item: algorithms, data model and metrics for goodness. Manual definition of request and result interpretation used on the current data mining tools may decrease with increase in automation. As the data mining applications are of diverse types, development of a "complete" data mining model is desirable. A major development will be in creation of a sophisticated "query language" that includes everything form SQL functions to the data mining applications.

A data mining query language (DMQL) based on SQL has been proposed. Difference between these two are:

TABLE 5.2 ***Difference between SQL and DMQL***

SQL	*DMQL*
Allows access only to relational database	Allows access to background information such as concept hierarchies
Here the retrieved data is necessarily an aggregate of data from relations	It indicates the type of knowledge to be mined and the retrieved data need not be a subset of data form relations
There is no such threshold level	It fixes a threshold that any mined information should obey

A BNF statement of DMQL can be given as modified from zaigg

<DMQL>:

USE DATABASE (database name)
{USE HIERARCHY <hierarchy name> FOR <attribute>}
<rule_spec>
RELATED TO <attr_or_agg_list>
FROM <relation(s)>
[WHERE <condition>]
[ORDER BY <order_list>]
{with [<kinds_of>]THRESHOLD = <threshold_value>[FOR <attribute(s)>]}

The heart of a DMQL statement is the rule specification portion. This is where the true data mining request is made. The data mining request can be one of the following.

- A generalized relation: obtained by generating data from input data
- A characteristic rule: condition that is satisfied by almost all records in a target class.
- A discriminate rule: condition that is satisfied by a target class but is different from conditions satisfied in other classes
- Classification rule: set of rules used to classify data.

Two latest models that gain access via ad hoc data mining queries are:

(1) **KDDMS (Knowledge and Data Discover Management System):** It is expected to be the future generation of data mining systems that include not only data mining tools but also techniques to manage the underlying data, ensure its consistency and provide concurrency and recovery features.

(2) **CRISP-DM (Cross Industry Standard Process for Data Mining):** This is a new KDD process model applicable to many different applications. The model addresses all steps in

the KDD process, including the maintenance of the results of the data mining step. Life cycle of CRISP-DM model can be described as follows:

Assess (business understanding)
|
Access (data understanding)
|
Analyze (data preparation)
|
Act (modeling)
|
Automate (evaluation deployment)

5.3 DATA MINING PRODUCTS

TABLE 5.3 *Products of Data Mining*

Product	*Vendor*	*Functions*	*Techniques*	*Platforms*
4 Thought	Congnos Inc.	Prediction	Neural Network (MLP)	Windows
CART	Salford Systems	Classification	Dicision tree (CART)	CMS , MYS, Unix (linux), Windows
Clementine	SPSS Inc.	Association rules, classification, clustering factor analysis, forecasting, prediction, sequence discovery	Apriori, BIRCH, CARMA, Decision trees (C5.0, C&RT a variation of CART), k-means clustering, neural networks, rule induction (C5.0, GRI) regression (linear, logarithm)	HP/UX, IBM, AIX, Sun Solaris, Windows NT
DB Miner Analytical System	DB Miner Technologies Inc.	Association rules, classification, clustering	Decision trees, k-means	Windows
Intelligent Miner	IBM Corporation	Association rules, clustering, classification, prediction sequential patterns, time series	Decision trees, k-means, neural networks (MLP, back propagation) regression (Linear)	Windows, Solaris, AIX, OS/390. OS/400
JDA Intellect	IDA Software Group	Association rules, classification, clustering, prediction	Naïve bayes, decision trees, k-means , k-nearest neighbour, neural networks (back-probagation , RBF)	Solaris, Windows

(*Contd...*)

Product	*Vendor*	*Functions*	*Techniques*	*Platforms*
MARS	Salford Systems	Forecasting	Regression	Unix(Linux, Solaris), Windows
Oracle 9i database	Oracle Corporation	Association rules, classification, prediction	Naïve bayes	All platforms on which oracle9i runs
s-plus	Insightful Corporation	Classification, clustering, hypothesis testing, prediction, time series analysis	ARIMA, correlation(Pearson), decision trees, hierarchical clustering(agglomerative, divisive), *k*-means, regression (linear, logistic, nonlinear, polynomial) statistical techniques (jackknife, Monte karlo)	Unix, Windows
Data Miner	Statsoft Inc.	Classification, clustering, prediction,	ARIMA, decision trees (CART, CHAID), exponential smoothing, neural networks(back-propagation, MLP, RBF, SOM), regression	Windows
Xpert Rule Miner	Attar Software Ltd	Association rules, classification, clustering	Decision trees, rules	ODBC, Windows

EXERCISE

1. List a few industries which apply data mining for the management of its vast database.
2. How does data mining help the banking industry?
3. List some of the applications of data dredging in managing scientific data.
4. What are the uses of data mining tools in *e*-commerce?
5. What is the real life application of data mining in the insurance industry?
6. Analyse the future scopes of data harvesting in the marketing industry.
7. List some of the products of data mining.

CHAPTER 6

DATA WAREHOUSE EVALUATION

6.1 THE CALCULATIONS FOR MEMORY CAPACITY

The past couple of decades have seen a dramatic increase in the amount of information or data being stored in electronic format. This accumulation of data has taken place at an explosive rate. It has been estimated that the amount of information in the world doubles every 20 months and the sizes as well as number of databases are increasing even faster. There are many examples that can be cited. Point of sale data in retail, policy and claim data in insurance, medical history data in health care, financial data in banking and securities, are some instances of the types of data that is being collected. Here, we are listed some interesting examples of data storage.

1. **Bytes** (8 bits)
   - 0.1 bytes: A binary decision
   - 1 byte: A single character
   - 10 bytes: A single word
   - 100 bytes: A telegram **OR** A punched card

2. **Kilobyte** (1000 bytes)
   - 1 Kilobyte: A very short story
   - 2 Kilobytes: A Typewritten page
   - 10 Kilobytes: An encyclopaedic page **OR** A deck of punched cards
   - 50 Kilobytes: A compressed document image page
   - 100 Kilobytes: A low-resolution photograph
   - 200 Kilobytes: A box of punched cards
   - 500 Kilobytes: A very heavy box of punched cards

3. **Megabyte** (1 000 000 bytes)
   - 1 Megabyte: A small novel **OR** A 3.5 inch floppy disk
   - 2 Megabytes: A high resolution photograph

- 5 Megabytes: The complete works of Shakespeare **OR** 30 seconds of TV-quality video
- 10 Megabytes: A minute of high-fidelity sound **OR** A digital chest X-ray
- 20 Megabytes: A box of floppy disks
- 50 Megabytes: A digital mammogram
- 100 Megabytes: 1 meter of shelved books **OR** A two-volume encyclopaedic book
- 200 Megabytes: A reel of 9-track tape **OR** An IBM 3480 cartridge tape
- 500 Megabytes: A CD-ROM

4. **Gigabyte** (1 000 000 000 bytes)

- 1 Gigabyte: A pickup truck filled with paper **OR** A symphony in high-fidelity sound **OR** A movie at TV quality
- 2 Gigabytes: 20 meters of shelved books **OR** A stack of 9-track tapes
- 5 Gigabytes: An 8mm Exabyte tape
- 10 Gigabytes:
- 20 Gigabytes: A good collection of the works of Beethoven
- 50 Gigabytes: A floor of books **OR** Hundreds of 9-track tapes
- 100 Gigabytes: A floor of academic journals **OR** A large ID-1 digital tape
- 200 Gigabytes: 50 Exabyte tapes

5. **Terabyte** (1 000 000 000 000 bytes)

- 1 Terabyte: An automated tape robot **OR** All the X-ray films in a large technological hospital **OR** 50000 trees made into paper and printed **OR** Daily rate of EOS data (1998)
- 2 Terabytes: An academic research library **OR** A cabinet full of Exabyte tapes
- 10 Terabytes: The printed collection of the US Library of Congress
- 50 Terabytes: The contents of a large Mass Storage System

6. **Petabyte** (1 000 000 000 000 000 bytes)

- 1 Petabyte: 3 years of EOS data (2001)
- 2 Petabytes: All US academic research libraries
- 20 Petabytes: Production of hard-disk drives in 1995
- 200 Petabytes: All printed material **OR** Production of digital magnetic tape in 1995

7. **Exabyte** (1 000 000 000 000 000 000 bytes)

- 5 Exabytes: All words ever spoken by human beings.

8. **Zettabyte** (1 000 000 000 000 000 000 000 bytes)
9. **Yottabyte** (1 000 000 000 000 000 000 000 000 bytes)

6.2 DATA, INFORMATION AND KNOWLEDGE

In this section we will present three terms widely—but often unreflectingly—used in several IT-related (and other) communities, *i.e.*, 'data', 'information', and 'knowledge'.

Data means any symbolic reperesentation of facts or ideas from which information can potentially be extracted. **Information** is a meaningful data and **Knowledge** is a interesting and useful patterns in a data base.

The definitions will be oriented according to the three dimensions of semiotics (the theory of signs), *i.e.*, syntax, semantics, and pragmatics.

"There is, in general, no known way to distinguish knowledge from information or data on a purely representational basis."

(1) The relation among signs, *i.e.*, the syntax of 'sentences' does not relate signs to anything in the real world and thus, can be called one-dimensional. In our eyes, signs only viewed under this dimension equal **data**.

(2) The relation between signs and their meaning, *i.e.*, their semantics adds a second dimension to signs. It is only through this relation between sign and meaning, that data becomes **information**.

(3) The third dimension is added by relating signs and their 'users'. If this third dimension including users, who pursue goals which require performing actions, is introduced, we call the patterns, or signs **knowledge**.

This relationship, which is called pragmatics, defines an important characteristic of knowledge, *i.e.*, only knowledge enables actions and decisions, performed by actors.

6.3 FUNDAMENTAL OF DATABASE

6.3.1 Definitions

A *database* is a collection of tables, with related data. Table 6.1 Provides Example of Employee table with 2 columns and 3 rows.

TABLE 6.1 *Example for Database*

Emp. number	*Name*
101	John
102	Jill
103	Jack

A *table* is a matrix with data. A table in a database looks like a simple spreadsheet. The example above has 3 rows and 2 columns in employee table.

One *column* (data element) contains data of one and the same kind, for example the column Emp_Number.

A *row* (= tuple, entry) is a group of related data, for example the data of one employee detail.

Normalization in a relational database is the process of removing redundancy in data by separating the data into multiple tables.

The process of removing redundancy in data by separating the data into multiple tables.

6.3.2 Data Base Design

Database design is the process of transforming a logical data model into an actual physical database. A logical data model is required before you can even begin to design a physical database. Assuming that the logical data model is complete, though, what must be done to implement a physical database?

The first step is to create an initial physical data model by transforming the logical data model into a physical implementation based on an understanding of the DBMS to be used for deployment. To successfully create a physical database design you will need to have a good working knowledge of the features of the DBMS including:

- In-depth knowledge of the database objects supported by the DBMS and the physical structures and files required to support those objects.
- Details regarding the manner in which the DBMS supports indexing, referential integrity, constraints, data types, and other features that augment the functionality of database objects.
- Detailed knowledge of new and obsolete features for particular versions or releases of the DBMS to be used.
- Knowledge of the DBMS configuration parameters that are in place.
- Data definition language (DDL) skills to translate the physical design into actual database objects.

Armed with the correct information, you can create an effective and efficient database from a logical data model. The first step in transforming a logical data model into a physical model is to perform a simple translation from logical terms to physical objects. Of course, this simple transformation will not result in a complete and correct physical database design – it is simply the first step. The transformation consists of the following:

- Transforming entities into tables
- Transforming attributes into columns
- Transforming domains into data types and constraints

To support the mapping of attributes to table columns you will need to map each logical domain of the attribute to a physical data type and perhaps additional constraints. In a physical database, each column must be assigned a **data type**. Certain data types require a maximum length to be specified. For example a character data type could be specified as VARCHAR(10), indicating that up to 10 characters can be stored for the column. You may need to apply a length to other data types as well, such as graphic, floating point, and decimal (which require a length and scale) types.

But no commercial DBMS product supports relational domains. Therefore the domain assigned in the logical data model must be mapped to a data type supported by the DBMS. You may need to adjust the data type based on the DBMS you use. For example, what data type and length will be used for monetary values if no built-in currency data type exists? Many of the major DBMS products support user-defined data types, so you might want to consider creating a data type to support the logical domain, if no built-in data type is acceptable.

In addition to a data type and length, you also may need to apply a constraint to the column. Consider a domain of integers between 1 and 10 inclusive. Simply assigning the physical column to an integer data type is insufficient to match the domain. A constraint must be added to restrict the values that can be stored for the column to the specified range, 1 through 10. Without a constraint, negative numbers, zero, and values greater than ten could be stored. Using **check** constraints you can place limits on the data values that can be stored in a column or set of columns.

Specification of a **primary key** is an integral part of the physical design of entities and attributes. A primary key should be assigned for every entity in the logical data model. As a first course of action you should try to use the primary key as selected in the logical data model. However, multiple candidate keys often are uncovered during the data modeling process. You may decide to choose a primary key other than the one selected during logical design – either one of the candidate keys or another surrogate key for physical implementation. But even if the DBMS does not mandate a primary key for each table it is a good practice to identify a primary key for each physical table you create. Failure to do so will make processing the data in that table more difficult.

Of course, there are many other decisions that must be made during the transition from logical to physical. For example, each of the following must be addressed:

- The nullability (NULL) of each column in each table.
- For character columns, should fixed length or variable length be used?
- Should the DBMS be used to assign values to sequences or identity columns?
- Implementing logical relationships by assigning referential constraints.
- Building indexes on columns to improve query performance.
- Choosing the type of index to create: b-tree, bit map, reverse key, hash, partitioning, etc.
- Deciding on the clustering sequence for the data.
- Other physical aspects such as column ordering, buffer pool specification, data files, de normalization, and so on.

6.3.3 Selection for the Database/Hardware Platform

RDBMS are used in OLTP applications (*e.g.*, ATM cards) very frequently and sometimes data warehouse may also use relational databases. Popular RDBMS Databases are listed below.

TABLE 6.2 *Packages—Example*

RDBMS name	*Company name*
Oracle	Oracle Corporation
IBM DB2 UDB	IBM Corporation
IBM Informix	IBM Corporation
Microsoft SQL Server	Microsoft
Sybase	Sybase Corporation
Terradata	NCR

In making selection for the database/hardware platform, there are several items that need to be carefully considered:

Scalability: How can the system grow as your data storage needs grow? Which RDBMS and hardware platform can handle large sets of data most efficiently? To get an idea of this, one needs to determine the approximate amount of data that is to be kept in the data warehouse system once it's mature, and base any testing numbers from there.

Parallel Processing Support: The days of multi-million dollar supercomputers with one single CPU are gone, and nowadays the most powerful computers all use multiple CPUs, where each processor can perform a part of the task, all at the same time. Massively parallel computers in 1993,so that it would be the best way for any large computations to be done within 5 years.

RDBMS/Hardware Combination: Because the RDBMS physically sits on the hardware platform, there are going to be certain parts of the code that is hardware platform-dependent. As a result, bugs and bug fixes are often hardware dependent.

6.4 OLAP AND OLAP SERVER

6.4.1 OLAP Definition

On-Line Analytical Processing (OLAP) is a category of software technology that enables analysts, managers and executives to gain insight into data through fast, consistent, interactive access to a wide variety of possible views of information that has been transformed from raw data to reflect the real dimensionality of the enterprise as understood by the user. OLAP functionality is characterized by dynamic multi-dimensional analysis of consolidated enterprise data supporting end user analytical and navigational activities including:

- calculations and modeling applied across dimensions, through hierarchies and/or across members
- trend analysis over sequential time periods
- slicing subsets for on-screen viewing
- drill-down to deeper levels of consolidation
- reach-through to underlying detail data
- rotation to new dimensional comparisons in the viewing area

OLAP is implemented in a multi-user client/server mode and offers consistently rapid response to queries, regardless of database size and complexity. OLAP helps the user synthesize enterprise information through comparative, personalized viewing, as well as through analysis of historical and projected data in various "what-if" data model scenarios. This is achieved through use of an OLAP server.

6.4.2 OLAP Server

An OLAP server is a high-capacity, multi-user data manipulation engine specifically designed to support and operate on multi-dimensional data structures. A multi-dimensional structure is arranged so that every data item is located and accessed based on the intersection of the dimension members which define that item. The design of the server and the structure of the data are optimized for rapid ad-hoc information retrieval in any orientation, as well as for fast, flexible calculation and transformation of raw data based on formulaic relationships. The OLAP server may either physically stage the processed multi-dimensional information to deliver consistent and rapid response times to end users, or it may populate its data structures in real-time from relational or other databases, or offer a choice of both. Given the current state of technology and the end user requirement for consistent and rapid response times, staging the multi-dimensional data in the OLAP server is often the preferred method.

6.5 DATA WAREHOUSES, OLTP, OLAP AND DATA MINING

A relational database is designed for a specific purpose. Because the purpose of a data warehouse differs from that of an On Line Transaction Processing (OLTP), the design characteristics of a relational database that supports a data warehouse differ from the design characteristics of an OLTP database.

An OLTP system is designed to handle a large volume of small-predefined transactions.

TABLE 6.3 ***Comparison of Data Warehouse Database and OLTP***

Data warehouse database	*OLTP database*
Designed for analysis of business measures by categories and attributes	Designed for real-time business operations
Optimized for bulk loads and large, complex, unpredictable queries that access many rows per table	Optimized for a common set of transactions, usually adding or retrieving a single row at a time per table
Loaded with consistent, valid data; requires no real time validation	Optimized for validation of incoming data during transactions; uses validation data tables
Supports few concurrent users relative to OLTP	Supports thousands of concurrent users

6.5.1 A Data Warehouse Supports OLTP

A data warehouse supports an OLTP system by providing a place for the OLTP database to offload data as it accumulates, and by providing services that would complicate and degrade OLTP operations if they were performed in the OLTP database.

Without a data warehouse to hold historical information, data is archived to static media such as magnetic tape, or allowed to accumulate in the OLTP database.

If data is simply archived for preservation, it is not available or organized for use by analysts and decision makers. If data is allowed to accumulate in the OLTP so it can be used for analysis, the OLTP database continues to grow in size and requires more indexes to service analytical and report queries. These queries access and process large portions of the continually growing historical data and add a substantial load to the database. The large indexes needed to support these queries also tax the OLTP transactions with additional index maintenance. These queries can also be complicated to develop due to the typically complex OLTP database schema.

A data warehouse offloads the historical data from the OLTP, allowing the OLTP to operate at peak transaction efficiency. High volume analytical and reporting queries are handled by the data warehouse and do not load the OLTP, which does not need additional indexes for their support. As data is moved to the data warehouse, it is also reorganized and consolidated so that analytical queries are simpler and more efficient.

6.5.2 OLAP is a Data Warehouse Tool

Online analytical processing (OLAP) is a technology designed to provide superior performance for ad hoc business intelligence queries. OLAP is designed to operate efficiently with data organized in accordance with the common dimensional model used in data warehouses.

A data warehouse provides a multidimensional view of data in an intuitive model designed to match the types of queries posed by analysts and decision makers. OLAP organizes data warehouse data into multidimensional cubes based on this dimensional model, and then preprocesses these cubes to provide maximum performance for queries that summarize data in various ways. For example, a query that requests the total sales income and quantity sold for a range of products in a specific geographical region for a specific time period can typically be answered in a few seconds or less regardless of how many hundreds of millions of rows of data are stored in the data warehouse database.

OLAP is not designed to store large volumes of text or binary data, nor is it designed to support high volume update transactions. The inherent stability and consistency of historical data in a data warehouse enables OLAP to provide its remarkable performance in rapidly summarizing information for analytical queries.

In SQL server 2000, Analysis Services provides tools for developing OLAP applications and a server specifically designed to service OLAP queries.

Other tolls are informatica, business objects and data stage.

6.5.3 Data Mining is a Data Warehouse Tool

Data mining is a technology that applies sophisticated and complex algorithms to analyze data and expose interesting information for analysis by decision makers. Whereas OLAP organizes data in a model suited for exploration by analysts, data mining performs analysis on data and provides the results to decision makers. Thus, OLAP supports model-driven analysis and data mining supports data-driven analysis.

Data mining has traditionally operated only on raw data in the data warehouse database or, more commonly, text files of data extracted from the data warehouse database. In SQL server 2000, analysis services provides data mining technology that can analyze data in OLAP cubes, as well as data in the relational data warehouse database. In addition, data mining results can be incorporated into OLAP cubes to further enhance model-driven analysis by providing an additional dimensional viewpoint into the OLAP model. For example, data mining can be used to analyze sales data against customer attributes and create a new cube dimension to assist the analyst in the discovery of the information embedded in the cube data.

6.5.4 Difference between OLTP and OLAP

TABLE 6.4 ***Difference between OLTP and OLAP***

	OLTP	*OLAP*
users	clerk, IT professional	knowledge worker
function	day to day operations	decision support
DB design	application-oriented	subject-oriented
data	current, up-to-date detailed, flat relational isolated	historical, summarized, multidimensional integrated consolidated
usage	repetitive	ad-hoc
access	read/write index/hash on prim, key	lots of scans
unit of work	short, simple transaction	complex query
# records accessed	tens	millions
# users	thousands	hundreds
DB size	100MB–GB	100GB–TB
metric	transaction throughout	query throughout, response

EXERCISE

1. What is the difference between data and information?
2. What are OLAP and OLAP Server?
3. What is OLTP?
4. What are the items to be considered to create a data warehouse?
5. Compare OLAP and OLTP.
6. Distinguish between data base warehouse and OLTP data base.

CHAPTER 7

DATA WAREHOUSE DESIGN

7.1 INTRODUCTION

Data Warehouse (DW) is a database that stores information oriented to satisfy decision-making requests. A very frequent problem in enterprises is the impossibility for accessing to corporate, complete and integrated information of the enterprise that can satisfy decision-making requests. A paradox occurs: data exists but information cannot be obtained. In general, a DW is constructed with the goal of storing and providing all the relevant information that is generated along the different databases of an enterprise. A DW is a database with particular features. Concerning the data it contains, it is the result of transformations, quality improvement and integration of data that comes from operational bases. Besides, it includes indicators that are derived from operational data and give it additional value. Concerning its utilization, it is supposed to support complex queries (summarization, aggregates, crossing of data), while its maintenance does not suppose transactional load. In addition, in a DW environment end users make queries directly against the DW through user-friendly query tools, instead of accessing information through reports generated by specialists.

Building and maintaining a DW need to solve problems of many different aspects. In this chapter we concentrate in DW design. A data warehouse has three main components:

- A "Central Data Warehouse" or "Operational Data Store(ODS)", which is a data base organized according to the corporate data model.
- One or more "data marts"—extracts from the central data warehouse that are organized according to the particular retrieval requirements of individual users.
- The "legacy systems" where an enterprise's data are currently kept.

7.2 THE CENTRAL DATA WAREHOUSE

The Central Data Warehouse is just that—a warehouse. All the enterprise's data are stored in there, "normalized", in order to minimize redundancy and so that each may be found easily. This is accomplished by organizing it according to the enterprise's corporate data model. Think of it as a giant grocery store warehouse where the chocolates are kept in one section, the T-shirt is in another, and the CDs are in a third. We found in the literature, globally two different approaches for Relational DW design: one that applies *dimensional modeling* techniques, and another that bases mainly in the concept of *materialized views*.

Dimensional models represent data with a "cube" structure, making more compatible logical data representation with OLAP data management. According to the objectives of dimensional modeling are:

(*i*) To produce database structures that are easy for end-users to understand and write queries against,

(*ii*) To maximize the efficiency of queries.

It achieves these objectives by minimizing the number of tables and relationships between them. Normalized databases have some characteristics that are appropriate for OLTP systems, but not for DWs:

(*i*) Its structure is not easy for end-users to understand and use. In OLTP systems this is not a problem because, usually end-users interact with the database through a layer of software.

(*ii*) Data redundancy is minimized. This maximizes efficiency of updates, but tends to penalize retrievals. Data redundancy is not a problem in DWs because data is not updated on-line.

The basic concepts of dimensional modeling are: *facts*, *dimensions* and *measures*. A *fact* is a collection of related data items, consisting of measures and context data. It typically represents business items or business transactions. A *dimension* is a collection of data that describe one business dimension. Dimensions determine the contextual background for the facts; they are the parameters over which we want to perform OLAP. A *measure* is a numeric attribute of a fact, representing the performance or behavior of the business relative to the dimensions.

OLAP cube design requirements will be a natural outcome of the dimensional model if the data warehouse is designed to support the way users wants to query data.

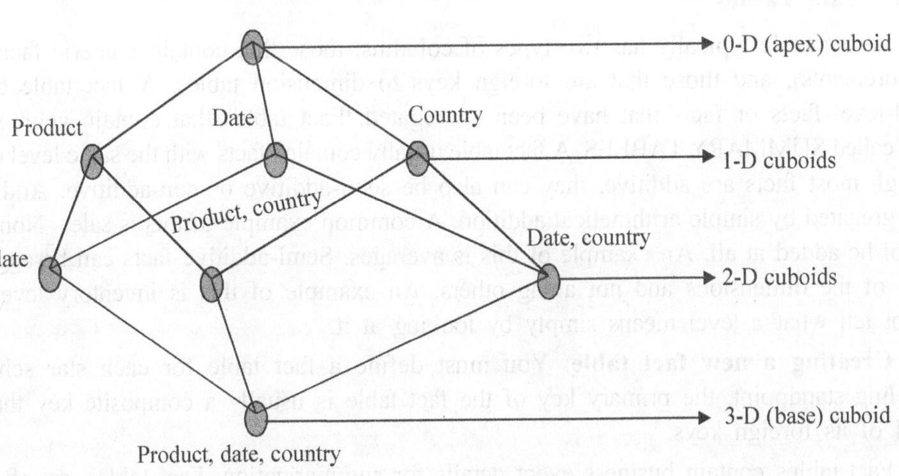

Fig. 7.1 Cubes

7.3 DATA WAREHOUSING OBJECTS

The following types of objects are commonly used in dimensional data warehouse schemas:

Fact tables are the large tables in your warehouse schema that store business measurements. Fact tables typically contain facts and foreign keys to the dimension tables. Fact tables represent data, usually numeric and additive, that can be analyzed and examined. Examples include sales, cost, and profit.

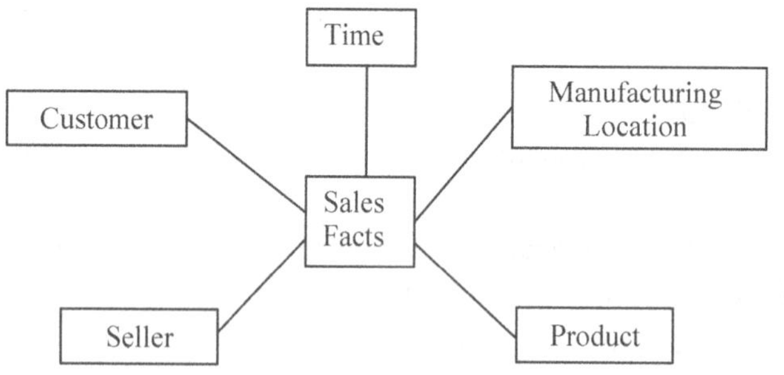

Fig. 7.2 A sales analysis star schema

Dimension tables, also known as **lookup** or **reference tables**, contain the relatively static data in the warehouse. Dimension tables store the information you normally use to contain queries. Dimension tables are usually textual and descriptive and you can use them as the row headers of the result set. Examples are *customers, Location, Time, Suppliers or products.*

7.3.1 Fact Tables

A fact table typically has two types of columns: those that contain numeric facts (often called measurements), and those that are foreign keys to dimension tables. A fact table contains either detail-level facts or facts that have been aggregated. Fact tables that contain aggregated facts are often called SUMMARY TABLES. A fact table usually contains facts with the same level of aggregation. Though most facts are additive, they can also be semi-additive or non-additive. Additive facts can be aggregated by simple arithmetical addition. A common example of this is sales. Non-additive facts cannot be added at all. An example of this is averages. Semi-additive facts can be aggregated along some of the dimensions and not along others. An example of this is inventory levels, where you cannot tell what a level means simply by looking at it.

Creating a new fact table: You must define a fact table for each star schema. From a modeling standpoint, the primary key of the fact table is usually a composite key that is made up of all of its foreign keys.

Fact tables contain business event details for summarization. Fact tables are often very large, containing hundreds of millions of rows and consuming hundreds of gigabytes or multiple terabytes of storage. Because dimension tables contain records that describe facts, the fact table can be reduced to columns for dimension foreign keys and numeric fact values. Text, BLOBs, and denormalized data are typically not stored in the fact table. The definitions of this 'sales' fact table follow:

```
CREATE TABLE sales
(
prod_id NUMBER(7) CONSTRAINT sales_product_nn NOT NULL,
cust_id NUMBER CONSTRAINT sales_customer_nn NOT NULL,
time_id DATE CONSTRAINT sales_time_nn NOT NULL,
ad_id NUMBER(7),quantity_sold NUMBER(4) CONSTRAINT sales_quantity_nn
NOT NULL,
amount NUMBER(10,2) CONSTRAINT sales_amount_nn NOT NULL,
cost NUMBER(10,2) CONSTRAINT sales_cost_nn NOT NULL )
```

Multiple Fact Tables: Multiple fact tables are used in data warehouses that address multiple business functions, such as sales, inventory, and finance. Each business function should have its own fact table and will probably have some unique dimension tables. Any dimensions that are common across the business functions must represent the dimension information in the same way, as discussed earlier in "Dimension Tables." Each business function will typically have its own schema that contains a fact table, several conforming dimension tables, and some dimension tables unique to the specific business function. Such business-specific schemas may be part of the central data warehouse or implemented as data marts.

Very large fact tables may be physically partitioned for implementation and maintenance design considerations. The partition divisions are almost always along a single dimension, and the time dimension is the most common one to use because of the historical nature of most data warehouse data. If fact tables are partitioned, OLAP cubes are usually partitioned to match the partitioned fact table segments for ease of maintenance. Partitioned fact tables can be viewed as one table with an SQL UNION query as long as the number of tables involved does not exceed the limit for a single query.

7.3.2 Dimension Tables

A dimension is a structure, often composed of one or more hierarchies, that categorizes data. Dimensional attributes help to describe the dimensional value. They are normally descriptive, textual values. Several distinct dimensions, combined with facts, enable you to answer business questions. Commonly used dimensions are customers, products, and time. Dimension data is typically collected at the lowest level of detail and then aggregated into higher-level totals that are more useful for analysis. These natural rollups or aggregations within a dimension table are called hierarchies.

A dimension table may be used in multiple places if the data warehouse contains multiple fact tables or contributes data to data marts. For example, a product dimension may be used with a sales fact table and an inventory fact table in the data warehouse, and also in one or more departmental data marts. A dimension such as customer, time, or product that is used in multiple schemas is called a *conforming dimension* if all copies of the dimension are the same. Summarization data and reports will not correspond if different schemas use different versions of a dimension table. Using conforming dimensions is critical to successful data warehouse design. The definitions of this 'customer' fact table follow:

```
CREATE TABLE customers
( cust_id NUMBER, cust_first_name VARCHAR2(20) CONSTRAINT customer_fname_nn NOT
NULL, cust_last_name VARCHAR2(40) CONSTRAINT customer_lname_nn NOT NULL,cust_sex
CHAR(1), cust_year_of_birth NUMBER(4), cust_marital_status VARCHAR2(20),cust_street_address
VARCHAR2(40) CONSTRAINT customer_st_addr_nn NOT NULL, cust_postal_code VARCHAR2(10)
CONSTRAINT customer_pcode_nn NOT NULL,cust_city VARCHAR2(30) CONSTRAINT
customer_city_nn NOT NULL, cust_state_district VARCHAR2(40),country_id CHAR(2)
CONSTRAINT customer_country_id_nn NOT NULL, cust_phone_number VARCHAR2(25),
cust_income_level VARCHAR2(30), cust_credit_limit NUMBER, cust_email VARCHAR2(30) )

CREATE DIMENSION products_dim
LEVEL product IS (products.prod_id)
LEVEL subcategory IS (products.prod_subcategory)
LEVEL category IS (products.prod_category)
HIERARCHY prod_rollup (
product CHILD OF
subcategory CHILD OF
category
)
ATTRIBUTE product DETERMINES products.prod_name
ATTRIBUTE product DETERMINES products.prod_desc
ATTRIBUTE subcategory DETERMINES products.prod_subcat_desc
ATTRIBUTE category DETERMINES products.prod_cat_desc;
```

The records in a dimension table establish one-to-many relationships with the fact table. For example, there may be a number of sales to a single customer, or a number of sales of a single product. The dimension table contains attributes associated with the dimension entry; these attributes are rich and user-oriented textual details, such as product name or customer name and address. Attributes serve as report labels and query constraints. Attributes that are coded in an OLTP database should be decoded into descriptions. For example, product category may exist as a simple integer in the OLTP database, but the dimension table should contain the actual text for the category. The code may also be carried in the dimension table if needed for maintenance. This denormalization simplifies and improves the efficiency of queries and simplifies user query tools. However, if a dimension attribute changes frequently, maintenance may be easier if the attribute is assigned to its own table to create a snowflake dimension.

Hierarchies: The data in a dimension is usually hierarchical in nature. Hierarchies are determined by the business need to group and summarize data into usable information. For example, a time dimension often contains the hierarchy elements: (all time), Year, Quarter, Month, Day or Week. A dimension may contain multiple hierarchies – a time dimension often contains both calendar and fiscal year hierarchies. Geography is seldom a dimension of its own; it is usually a hierarchy that imposes a structure on sales points, customers, or other geographically distributed dimensions. An example geography hierarchy for sales points is: (all), country, region, state or district, city, store.

Level relationships specify top-to-bottom ordering of levels from most general (the root) to most specific information. They define the parent-child relationship between the levels in a hierarchy. Hierarchies are also essential components in enabling more complex rewrites. For example, the database can aggregate existing sales revenue on a quarterly base to a yearly aggregation when the dimensional dependencies between quarter and year are known.

Multi-use dimensions: Sometimes data warehouse design can be simplified by combining a number of small, unrelated dimensions into a single physical dimension, often called a **junk dimension**. This can greatly reduce the size of the fact table by reducing the number of foreign keys in fact table records. Often the combined dimension will be prepopulated with the cartesian product of all dimension values. If the number of discrete values creates a very large table of all possible value combinations, the table can be populated with value combinations as they are encountered during the load or update process.

A common example of a multi-use dimension is a dimension that contains customer demographics selected for reporting standardization. Another multiuse dimension might contain useful textual comments that occur infrequently in the source data records; collecting these comments in a single dimension removes a sparse text field from the fact table and replaces it with a compact foreign key.

7.4 GOALS OF DATA WAREHOUSE ARCHITECTURE

A data warehouse exists to serve its users—analysts and decision makers. A data warehouse must be designed to satisfy the following requirements:

- Deliver a great user experience—user acceptance is the measure of success
- Function without interfering with OLTP systems
- Provide a central repository of consistent data
- Answer complex queries quickly
- Provide a variety of powerful analytical tools such as OLAP and data mining

Most successful data warehouses that meet these requirements have these common characteristics:

- Based on a dimensional model
- Contain historical data
- Include both detailed and summarized data
- Consolidate disparate data from multiple sources while retaining consistency
- Focus on a single subject such as sales, inventory, or finance

Data warehouses are often quite large. However, size is not an architectural goal—it is a characteristic driven by the amount of data needed to serve the users.

7.5 DATA WAREHOUSE USERS

The success of a data warehouse is measured solely by its acceptance by users. Without users, historical data might as well be archived to magnetic tape and stored in the basement. Successful data warehouse design starts with understanding the users and their needs.

Data warehouse users can be divided into four categories: Statisticians, knowledge workers, information consumers, and executives. Each type makes up a portion of the user population as illustrated in this diagram.

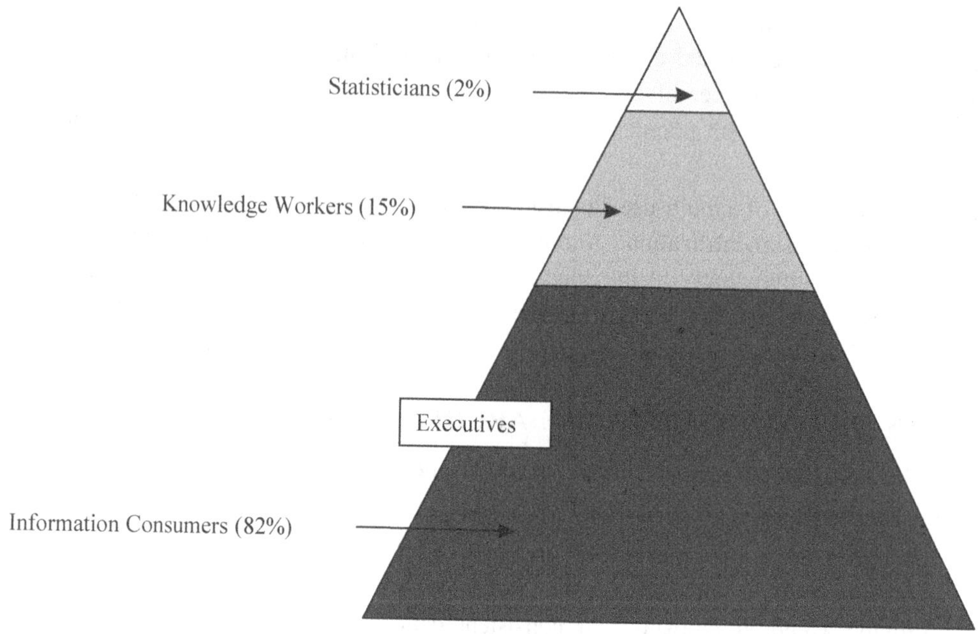

Fig. 7.3 Data warehouse users

Statisticians: There are typically only a handful of statisticians and operations research types in any organization. Their work can contribute to closed loop systems that deeply influence the operations and profitability of the company.

Knowledge Workers: A relatively small number of analysts perform the bulk of new queries and analyses against the data warehouse. These are the users who get the Designer or Analyst versions of user access tools. They will figure out how to quantify a subject area. After a few iterations, their queries and reports typically get published for the benefit of the Information Consumers. Knowledge Workers are often deeply engaged with the data warehouse design and place the greatest demands on the ongoing data warehouse operations team for training and support.

Information Consumers: Most users of the data warehouse are Information Consumers; they will probably never compose a true ad hoc query. They use static or simple interactive reports that others have developed. They usually interact with the data warehouse only through the work product of others. This group includes a large number of people, and published reports are highly visible. Set up a great communication infrastructure for distributing information widely, and gather feedback from these users to improve the information sites over time.

Executives: Executives are a special case of the Information Consumers group.

7.5.1 How Users Query the Data Warehouse?

Information for users can be extracted from the data warehouse relational database or from the output of analytical services such as OLAP or data mining. Direct queries to the data warehouse relational database should be limited to those that cannot be accomplished through existing tools, which are often more efficient than direct queries and impose less load on the relational database.

Reporting tools and custom applications often access the database directly. Statisticians frequently extract data for use by special analytical tools. Analysts may write complex queries to extract and compile specific information not readily accessible through existing tools. Information consumers do not interact directly with the relational database but may receive e-mail reports or access web pages that expose data from the relational database. Executives use standard reports or ask others to create specialized reports for them.

When using the analysis services tools in SQL server 2000, statisticians will often perform data mining, analysts will write MDX queries against OLAP cubes and use data mining, and Information Consumers will use interactive reports designed by others.

7.6 DESIGN THE RELATIONAL DATABASE AND OLAP CUBES

In this phase, the star or snowflake schema is created in the relational database, surrogate keys are defined and primary and foreign key relationships are established. Views, indexes, and fact table partitions are also defined. OLAP cubes are designed that support the needs of the users.

7.6.1 Keys and Relationships

Tables are implemented in the relational database after surrogate keys for dimension tables have been defined and primary and foreign keys and their relationships have been identified. Primary/foreign key relationships should be established in the database schema.. The composite primary key in the fact table is an expensive key to maintain. Integrity constraints provide a mechanism for ensuring that data conforms to guidelines specified by the database administrator. The most common types of constraints include:

- ✧ UNIQUE constraints—To ensure that a given column is unique
- ✧ NOT NULL constraints—To ensure that no null values are allowed
- ✧ FOREIGN KEY constraints—To ensure that two keys share a primary key to foreign key relationship

Constraints can be used for these purposes in a data warehouse is Data cleanliness and Query optimization. The index alone is almost as large as the fact table. The index on the primary key is often created as a clustered index. In many scenarios a clustered primary key provides excellent query performance. However, all other indexes on the fact table use the large clustered index key. All indexes on the fact table will be large, the system will require significant additional storage space, and query performance may degrade.

As a result, many star schemas are defined with an integer surrogate primary key, or no primary key at all. We recommend that the fact table be defined using the composite primary key. Also create an IDENTITY column in the fact table that could be used as a unique clustered index, should the database administrator determine this structure would provide better performance.

7.6.2 Indexes

Dimension tables must be indexed on their primary keys, which are the surrogate keys created for the data warehouse tables. The fact table must have a unique index on the primary key. There are scenarios where the primary key index should be clustered and other scenarios where it should not. The larger the number of dimensions in the schema, the less beneficial it is to cluster the primary key index. With a large number of dimensions, it is usually more effective to create a unique clustered index on a meaningless IDENTITY column.

Elaborate initial design and development of index plans for end-user queries is not necessary with SQL server 2000, which has sophisticated index techniques and an easy to use Index Tuning Wizard tool to tune indexes to the query workload.

The SQL Server 2000 Index Tuning Wizard allows you to select and create an optimal set of indexes and statistics for a database without requiring an expert understanding of the structure of the database, the workload, or the internals of SQL Server. The wizard analyzes a query workload captured in a SQL Profiler trace or provided by an SQL script, and recommends an index configuration to improve the performance of the database.

The index tuning wizard provides the following features and functionality:

- It can use the query optimizer to analyze the queries in the provided workload and recommend the best combination of indexes to support the query mix in the workload.
- It analyzes the effects of the proposed changes, including index usage, distribution of queries among tables, and performance of queries in the workload.
- It can recommend ways to tune the database for a small set of problem queries.
- It allows you to customize its recommendations by specifying advanced options, such as disk space constraints.

A recommendation from the wizard consists of SQL statements that can be executed to create new, more effective indexes and, if wanted, drop existing indexes that are ineffective. Indexed views are recommended on platforms that support their use. After the Index Tuning Wizard has suggested a recommendation, it can then be implemented immediately, scheduled as a SQL Server job, or executed manually at a later time.

The empirical tuning approach provided by the index tuning wizard can be used frequently when the data warehouse is first implemented to develop the initial index set, and then employed periodically during ongoing operation to maintain indexes in tune with the user query workload.

7.6.3 Views

Views should be created for users who need direct access to data in the data warehouse relational database. Users can be granted access to views without having access to the underlying data. Indexed views can be used to improve performance of user queries that access data through views. View definitions should create column and table names that will make sense to business users.

7.7 DATA WAREHOUSING SCHEMAS

A schema is a collection of database objects, including tables, views, indexes, and synonyms. You can arrange schema objects in the schema models designed for data warehousing in a variety of ways. Most data warehouses use a dimensional model. The model of your source data and the requirements of your users help you design the data warehouse schema. You can sometimes get the source model from your company's enterprise data model and reverse-engineer the logical data model for the data warehouse from this. The physical implementation of the logical data warehouse model may require some changes to adapt it to your system parameters—size of machine, number of users, storage capacity, type of network, and software.

7.7.1 Dimensional Model Schemas

The principal characteristic of a dimensional model is a set of detailed business facts surrounded by multiple dimensions that describe those facts. When realized in a database, the schema for a dimensional model contains a central fact table and multiple dimension tables. A dimensional model may produce a *star schema* or a *snowflake schema.*

7.7.1.1 Star Schemas

A schema is called a *star schema* if all dimension tables can be joined directly to the fact table. The following diagram shows a classic star schema. In the star schema design, a single object (the fact table) sits in the middle and is radically connected to other surrounding objects (dimension lookup tables) like a star. A star schema can be simple or complex. A simple star consists of one fact table; a complex star can have more than one fact table.

Steps in Designing Star Schema

- Identify a business process for analysis (like sales).
- Identify measures or facts (sales dollar).
- Identify dimensions for facts (product dimension, location dimension, time dimension, organization dimension).
- List the columns that describe each dimension (region name, branch name, subregion name).
- Determine the lowest level of summary in a fact table (sales dollar).

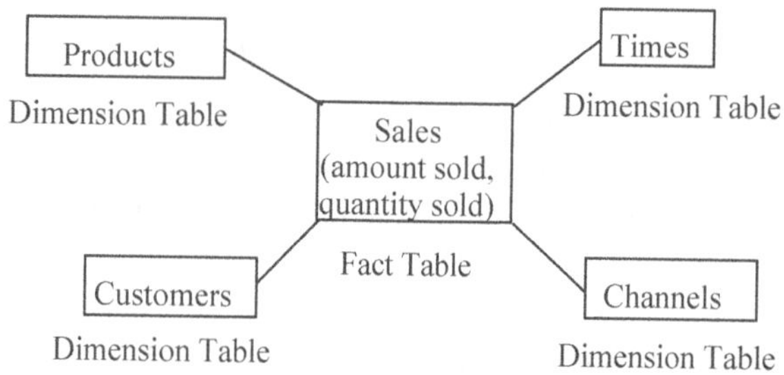

Fig. 7.4 Star schema

Example – Star Schema with Time Dimension

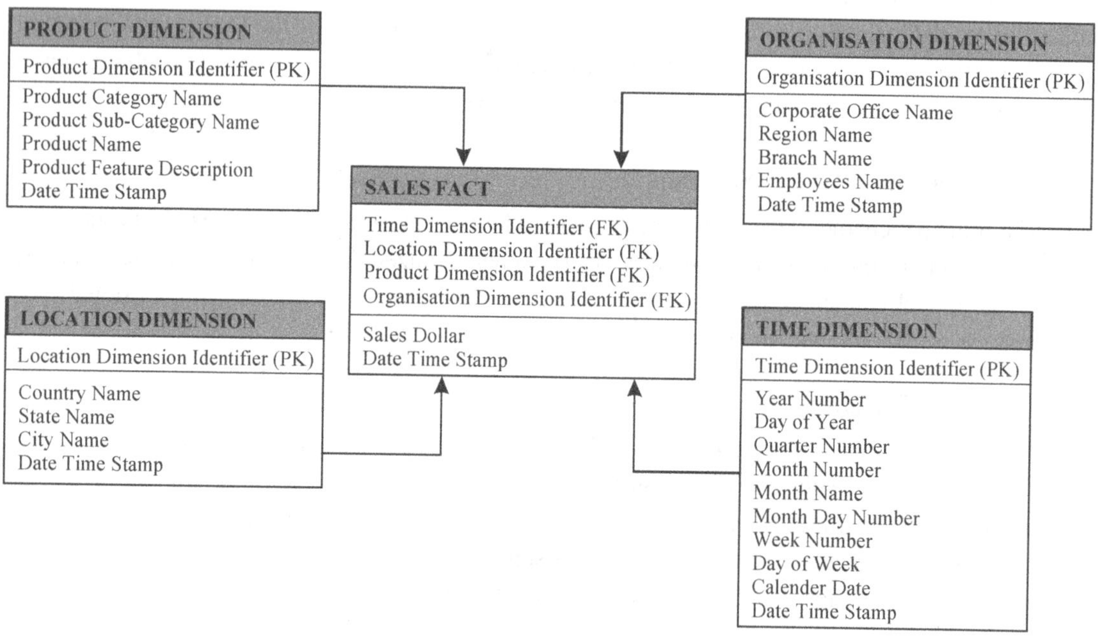

Fig. 7.5 Example of star schema

Hierarchy

A logical structure that uses ordered levels as a means of organizing data. A hierarchy can be used to define data aggregation; for example, in a time dimension, a hierarchy might be used to aggregate data from the month level to the quarter level, from the quarter level to the year level. A hierarchy can also be used to define a navigational drill path, regardless of whether the levels in the hierarchy represent aggregated totals or not.

Level

A position in a hierarchy. For example, a time dimension might have a hierarchy that represents data at the month, quarter, and year levels.

Fact Table

A table in a star schema that contains facts and connected to dimensions. A fact table typically has two types of columns: those that contain facts and those that are foreign keys to dimension tables. The primary key of a fact table is usually a composite key that is made up of all of its foreign keys.

A fact table might contain either detail level facts or facts that have been aggregated (fact tables that contain aggregated facts are often instead called summary tables). A fact table usually contains facts with the same level of aggregation.

In the example Fig. 7.6, sales fact table is connected to dimensions location, product, time and organization. It shows that data can be sliced across all dimensions and again it is possible for the data to be aggregated across multiple dimensions. "Sales Dollar" in sales fact table can be calculated across all dimensions independently or in a combined manner which is explained below.

- ✧ Sales dollar value for a particular product
- ✧ Sales dollar value for a product in a location
- ✧ Sales dollar value for a product in a year within a location
- ✧ Sales dollar value for a product in a year within a location sold or serviced by an employee

7.7.1.2 Snowflake Schemas

A schema is called a *snowflake schema* if one or more dimension tables do not join directly to the fact table but must join through other dimension tables. For example, a dimension that describes products may be separated into three tables (snowflaked).

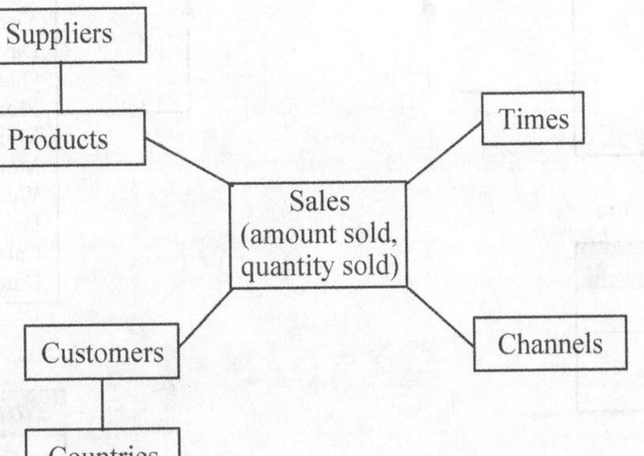

Fig. 7.6 A snowflake schema

The snowflake schema is an extension of the star schema where each point of the star explodes into more points. The main advantage of the snowflake schema is the improvement in query performance due to minimized disk storage requirements and joining smaller lookup tables. The main disadvantage of the snowflake schema is the additional maintenance efforts needed due to the increase number of lookup tables.

Example—Snowflake Schema

In Snowflake schema, the example diagram shown below has 4 dimension tables, 4 lookup tables and 1 fact table. The reason is that hierarchies(category, branch, state, and month) are being broken out of the dimension tables (PRODUCT, ORGANIZATION, LOCATION, and TIME)

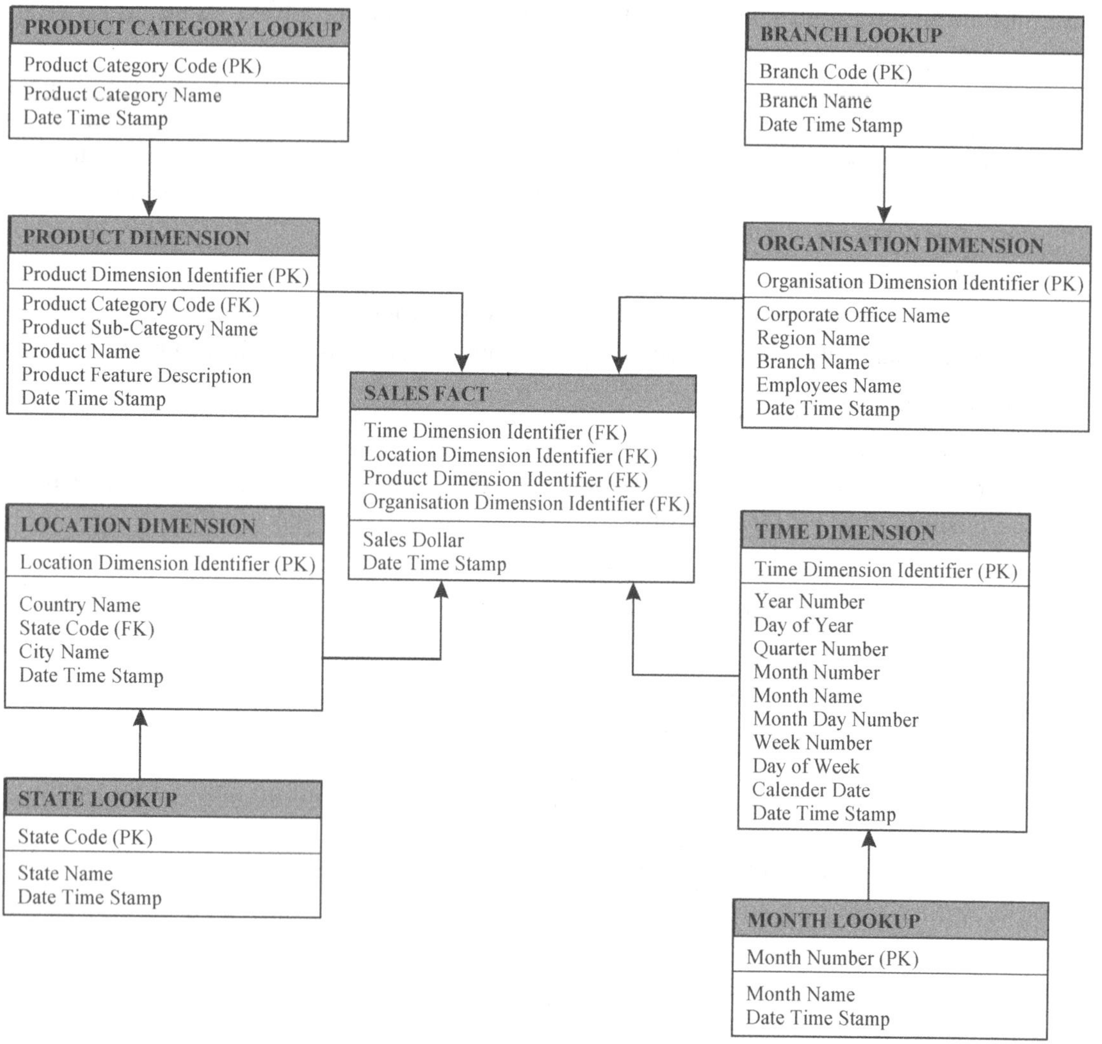

Fig. 7.7 Example of snowflake schema

respectively and shown separately. In OLAP, this Snowflake schema approach increases the number of joins and poor performance in retrieval of data. In few organizations, they try to normalize the dimension tables to save space. Since dimension tables hold less space, Snowflake schema approach may be avoided.

7.7.1.3 Important Aspects of Star Schema & Snowflake Schema

- ✧ In a star schema every dimension will have a primary key.
- ✧ In a star schema, a dimension table will not have any parent table.
- ✧ Whereas in a snowflake schema, a dimension table will have one or more parent tables.
- ✧ Hierarchies for the dimensions are stored in the dimensional table itself in star schema.
- ✧ Whereas hierarchies are broken into separate tables in snowflake schema. These hierarchies help to drill down the data from topmost hierarchies to the lowermost hierarchies.

EXERCISE

1. Write an essay on schemas.
2. Define fact and dimension tables.
3. Discuss about use of data warehouse.
4. Explain data warehouse architecture.
5. Who are data warehouse users? Explain.
6. How will you design OLAP cubes?

CHAPTER 8

PARTITIONING IN DATA WAREHOUSE

8.1 INTRODUCTION

Data warehouses often contain large tables and require techniques both for managing these large tables and for providing good query performance across these large tables. The objective of partitioning is manageability and performance related requirements.

These topics are discussed:

- Hardware partitioning
- Software partitioning

8.2 HARDWARE PARTITIONING

When a system is constrained by I/O capabilities, it is **I/O bottleneck**. When a system is constrained by having limited CPU resources, it is **CPU bottleneck**. Database architects frequently use RAID (Redundant Arrays of Inexpensive Disks) systems to overcome I/O bottlenecks and to provide higher availability. RAID can be implemented in several levels, ranging from 0 to 7.

RAID is a storage technology often used for databases larger than a few gigabytes. RAID can provide both performance and fault tolerance benefits. A variety of RAID controllers and disk configurations offer tradeoffs among cost, performance, and fault tolerance.

Performance

Hardware RAID controllers divide read/writes of all data from Windows NT 4.0 and Windows 2000 and applications (like SQL Server) into slices (usually 16–128 KB) that are then spread across all disks participating in the RAID array. Splitting data across physical drives like this has the effect of distributing the read/write I/O workload evenly across all physical hard drives participating in the RAID array. This increases disk I/O performance because the hard disks participating in the RAID array, as a whole are kept equally busy, instead of some disks becoming a bottleneck due to uneven distribution of the I/O requests.

Fault Tolerance

RAID also provides protection from hard disk failure and accompanying data loss by using two methods: mirroring and parity.

Mirroring

It is implemented by writing information onto a second (mirrored) set of drives. If there is a drive loss with mirroring in place, the data for the lost drive can be rebuilt by replacing the failed drive and rebuilding the mirror set. Most RAID controllers provide the ability to do this failed drive replacement and re-mirroring while Windows NT 4.0 and Windows 2000 and RDBMS are online. Such RAID systems are commonly referred to as "Hot Plug" capable drives.

Advantage

It offers the best performance among RAID options if fault tolerance is required. Bear in mind that each RDBMS write to the mirrorset results in two disk I/O operations, once to each side of the mirrorset. Another advantage is that mirroring provides more fault tolerance than parity RAID implementations. Mirroring can enable the system to survive at least one failed drive and may be able to support the system through failure of up to half of the drives in the mirrorset without forcing the system administrator to shut down the server and recover from the file backup.

Disadvantage

The disk cost of mirroring is one extra drive for each drive worth of data. This essentially doubles your storage cost, which, for a data warehouse, is often one of the most expensive components needed. Both RAID 1 and its hybrid, RAID 0+1 (sometimes referred to as RAID 10 or 0/1) are implemented through mirroring.

Parity

It is implemented by calculating recovery information about data written to disk and writing this parity information on the other drives that form the RAID array. If a drive should fail, a new drive is inserted into the RAID array and the data on that failed drive is recovered by taking the recovery information (parity) written on the other drives and using this information to regenerate the data from the failed drive. RAID 5 and its hybrids are implemented through parity.

Advantage

The main plus of parity is cost. To protect any number of drives with RAID 5, only one additional drive is required. Parity information is evenly distributed among all drives participating in the RAID 5 array.

Disadvantages

The minus of parity are performance and fault tolerance. Due to the additional costs associated with calculating and writing parity, RAID 5 requires four disk I/O operations for each write, compared to two disk I/O operations for mirroring. Read I/O operation costs are the same for mirroring and parity. Read operations, however, are usually one failed drive before the array must be taken offline and recovery from backup media must be performed to restore data.

General Rule of Thumb: Be sure to stripe across as many disks as necessary to achieve solid disk I/O performance. System monitor will indicate if there is a disk I/O bottleneck on a particular RAID array. Be ready to add disks and redistribute data across RAID arrays and/or small computer system interface (SCSI) channels as necessary to balance disk I/O and maximize performance.

Effect of On-Board Cache of Hardware RAID Controllers

Many hardware RAID controllers have some form of read and/or write caching. This available caching with SQL Server can significantly enhance the effective I/O handling capacity of the disk subsystem. The principle of these controller-based caching mechanisms is to gather smaller and potentially nonsequential I/O requests coming in from the host server and try to batch them together with other I/O requests for a few milliseconds so that the batched I/Os can form larger (32–128 KB) and maybe sequential I/O requests to send to the hard drives.

In keeping with the principle that sequential and larger I/O is good for performance, this helps produce more disk I/O throughput given the fixed number of I/Os that hard disks are able to provide to the RAID controller. It is not that the RAID controller caching magically allows the hard disks to process more I/Os per second. Rather, the RAID controller cache is using some organization to arrange incoming I/O requests to make best possible use of the underlying hard disks' fixed amount of I/O processing ability.

These RAID controllers usually protect their caching mechanism with some form of backup power. This backup power can help preserve the data written in cache for some period of time (perhaps days) in case of a power outage. If the database server is also supported by an uninterruptible power supply (UPS), the RAID controller has more time and opportunity to flush data to disk in the event of power disruption. Although a UPS for the server does not directly affect performance, it does provide protection for the performance improvement supplied by RAID controller caching.

8.3 RAID LEVELS

Level 0

This level is also known as disk striping because of its use of a disk file system called a stripe set. Data is divided into blocks and spread in a fixed order among all disks in an array. RAID 0 improves read/write performance by spreading operations across multiple disks, so that operations can be performed independently and simultaneously. RAID 0 is similar to RAID 5, except RAID 5 also provides fault tolerance. The following illustration shows RAID 0.

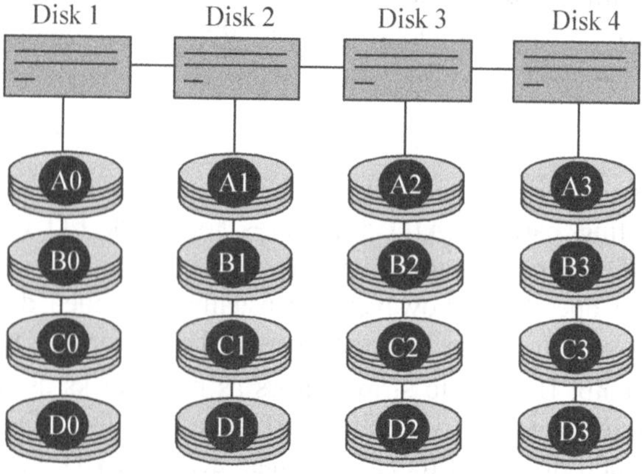

Fig. 8.1 RAID level 0

Level 1

This level is also known as disk mirroring because it uses a disk file system called a mirror set. Disk mirroring provides a redundant, identical copy of a selected disk. All data written to the primary disk is written to the mirror disk. RAID 1 provides fault tolerance and generally improves read performance (but may degrade write performance). The following illustration shows RAID 1.

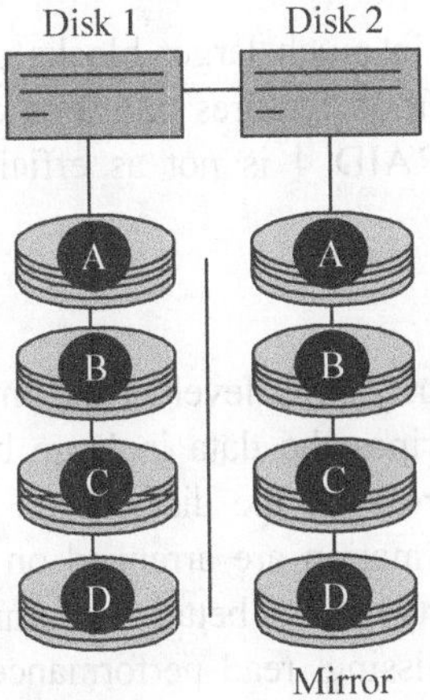

Fig. 8.2 RAID level 1

Level 2

This level adds redundancy by using an error correction method that spreads parity across all disks. It also employs a disk-striping strategy that breaks a file into bytes and spreads it across multiple disks. This strategy offers only a marginal improvement in disk utilization and read/write performance over mirroring (RAID 1). RAID 2 is not as efficient as other RAID levels and is not generally used.

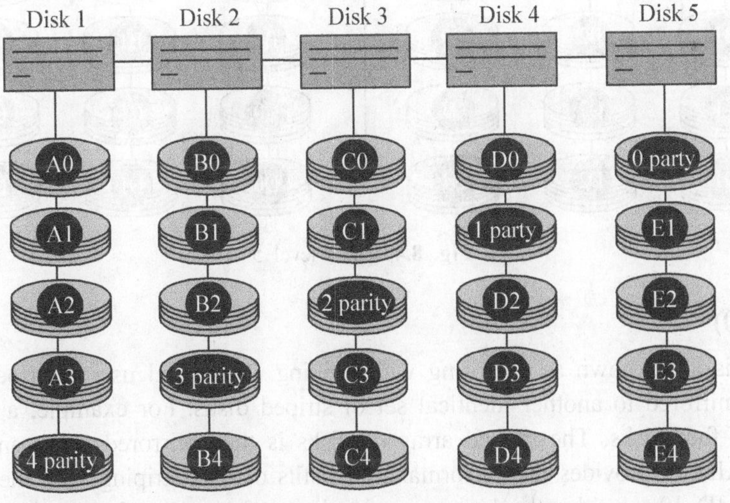

Fig. 8.3 RAID level 2

Level 3

This level uses the same striping method as RAID 2, but the error correction method requires only one disk for parity data. Use of disk space varies with the number of data disks. RAID 3 provides some read/write performance improvement. RAID 3 also is rarely used.

Level 4

This level employs striped data in much larger blocks or segments than RAID 2 or RAID 3. Like RAID 3, the error correction method requires only one disk for parity data. It keeps user data separate from error-correction data. RAID 4 is not as efficient as other RAID levels and is not generally used.

Level 5

Also known as striping with parity, this level is the most popular strategy for new designs. It is similar to RAID 4 because it stripes the data in large blocks across the disks in an array. It differs in how it writes the parity across all the disks. Data redundancy is provided by the parity information. The data and parity information are arranged on the disk array so the two are always on different disks. Striping with parity offers better performance than disk mirroring (RAID 1). However, when a stripe member is missing, read performance degrades (for example, when a disk fails). RAID 5 is one of the most commonly used RAID configurations. The following illustration shows RAID 5.

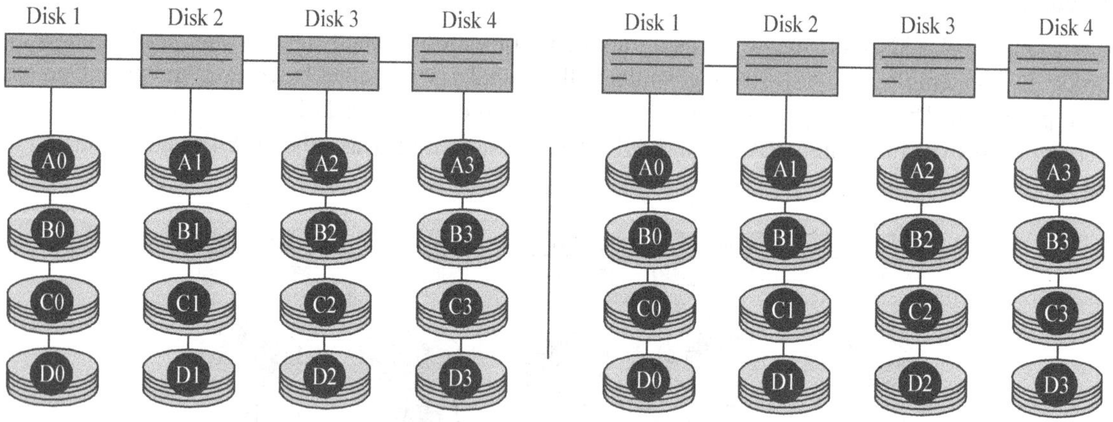

Fig. 8.4 RAID level 5

Level 10 (1 + 0)

This level is also known as mirroring with striping. This level uses a striped array of disks, which are then mirrored to another identical set of striped disks. For example, a striped array can be created using four disks. The striped array of disks is then mirrored using another set of four striped disks. RAID 10 provides the performance benefits of disk striping with the disk redundancy of mirroring. RAID 10 provides the highest read/write performance of any of the RAID levels at the expense of using twice as many disks. The following illustration shows RAID 10.

As mentioned above, RAID 1 and RAID 0+1 offer the best data protection and best performance among RAID levels, but cost more in terms of disks required. When cost of hard disks is not a limiting factor, RAID 1 or RAID 0+1 are the best choices in terms of both performance and fault tolerance.

RAID 5 costs less than RAID 1 or RAID 0+1 but provides less fault tolerance and less write performance. The write performance of RAID 5 is only about half that of RAID 1 or RAID 0+1 because of the additional I/O needed to read and write parity information.

The best disk I/O performance is achieved with RAID 0 (disk striping with no fault tolerance protection). Because RAID 0 provides no fault tolerance protection, it should never be used in a production environment, and it is not recommended for development environments. RAID 0 is typically used only for benchmarking or testing.

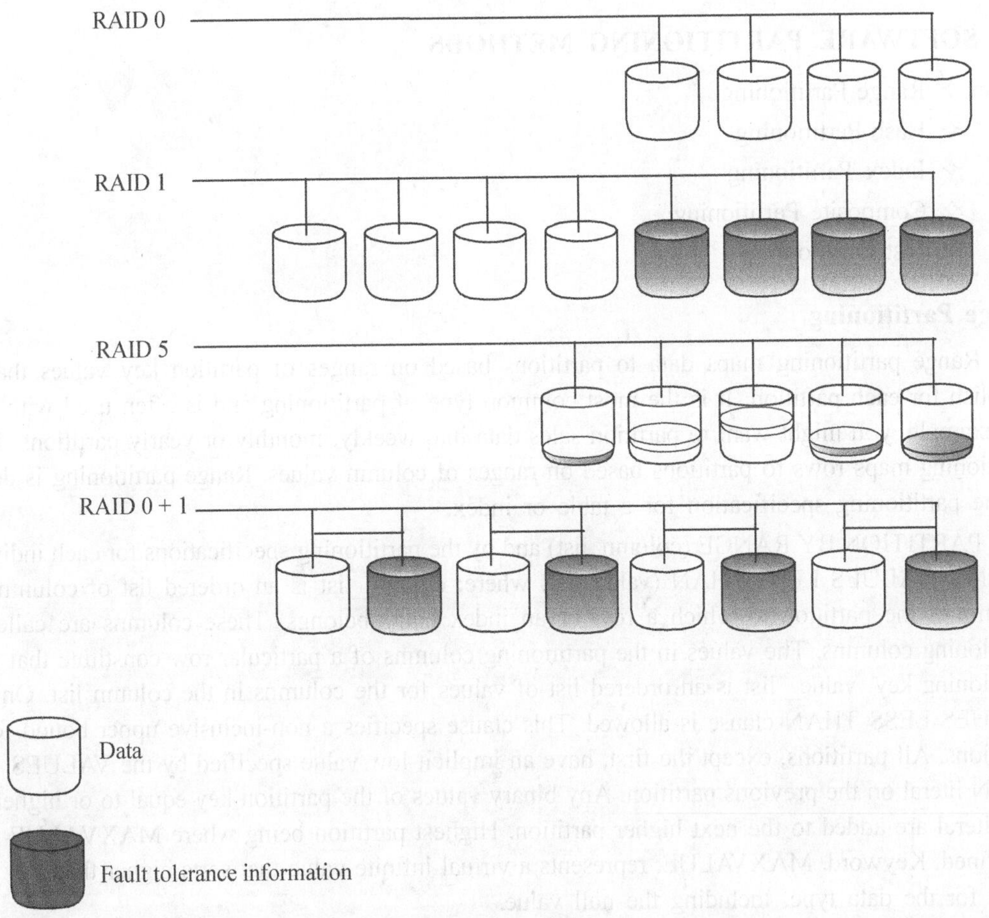

Fig. 8.5 Comparison of different RAID levels

Many RAID array controllers provide the option of RAID 0+1 (also referred to as RAID 1/0 and RAID 10) over physical hard drives. RAID 0+1 is a hybrid RAID solution. On the lower level, it mirrors all data just like normal RAID 1. On the upper level, the controller stripes data across all of the drives (like RAID 0). Thus, RAID 0+1 provides maximum protection (mirroring) with high performance (striping). These striping and mirroring operations are transparent to Windows and RDBMS because they are managed by the RAID controller. The difference between RAID 1 and RAID 0+1 is on the hardware controller level. RAID 1 and RAID 0+1 require the same number of drives for a given amount of storage. For more information on RAID 0+1 implementation of specific RAID controllers, contact the hardware vendor that produced the controller.

The Fig. 8.5 shows differences between RAID 0, RAID 1, RAID 5, and RAID 0+1.

Note: In the illustration above, in order to hold four disks worth of data, RAID 1 (and RAID 0+1) need eight disks, whereas Raid 5 only requires five disks. Be sure to involve your storage vendor to learn more about their specific RAID implementation.

8.4 SOFTWARE PARTITIONING METHODS

- ✧ Range Partitioning
- ✧ Hash Partitioning
- ✧ Index Partitioning
- ✧ Composite Partitioning
- ✧ List Partitioning

Range Partitioning

Range partitioning maps data to partitions based on ranges of partition key values that you establish for each partition. It is the most common type of partitioning and is often used with dates. For example, you might want to partition sales data into weekly, monthly or yearly partitions. Range partitioning maps rows to partitions based on ranges of column values. Range partitioning is defined by the partitioning specification for a table or index.

PARTITION BY RANGE (column_list) and by the partitioning specifications for each individual partition: VALUES LESS THAN (value_list) where: column_list is an ordered list of columns that determines the partition to which a row or an index entry belongs. These columns are called the partitioning columns. The values in the partitioning columns of a particular row constitute that row's partitioning key. value_ list is an ordered list of values for the columns in the column list. Only the VALUES LESS THAN clause is allowed. This clause specifies a non-inclusive upper bound for the partitions. All partitions, except the first, have an implicit low value specified by the VALUES LESS THAN literal on the previous partition. Any binary values of the partition key equal to or higher than this literal are added to the next higher partition. Highest partition being where MAXVALUE literal is defined. Keyword, MAXVALUE, represents a virtual infinite value that sorts higher than any other value for the data type, including the null value.

The statement below creates a table sales_range_part that is range partitioned on the sales_date field using Oracle.

```
CREATE TABLE sales_range_part
(sales_man_id NUMBER(6), emp_name VARCHAR2(25), sales_amount NUMBER(10),
sales_date DATE) PARTITION BY RANGE(sales_date) (
PARTITION sales_jan2006 VALUES LESS THAN(TO_DATE('02/01/2006','MM/DD/YYYY')),
PARTITION sales_feb2006 VALUES LESS THAN(TO_DATE('03/01/2006','MM/DD/YYYY')),
PARTITION sales_mar2006 VALUES LESS THAN(TO_DATE('04/01/2006','MM/DD/YYYY')),
PARTITION sales_apr2006 VALUES LESS THAN(TO_DATE('05/01/2006','MM/DD/YYYY')),);
```

Hash Partitioning

Hash partitioning maps data to partitions based on a hashing algorithm that Oracle applies to a partitioning key that you identify. The hashing algorithm evenly distributes rows among partitions, giving partitions approximately the same size. Hash partitioning is the ideal method for distributing data evenly across devices. Hash partitioning is a good and easy-to-use alternative to range partitioning when data is not historical and there is no obvious column or column list where logical range partition pruning can be advantageous. Oracle uses a linear hashing algorithm and to prevent data from clustering within specific partitions, you should define the number of partitions by a power of two (for example, 2, 4, 8). The statement below creates a table sales_hash, which is hash partitioned on the salesman_id field. datal, data2, data3, and data4 are tablespace names.

```
CREATE TABLE sales_hash
(salesman_id NUMBER(5), emp_name VARCHAR2(25), sales_amount NUMBER(10),
week_no NUMBER(2)) PARTITION BY HASH(salesman_id)
PARTITIONS 4 STORE IN (datal, data2, data3, data4);
```

List Partitioning

List partitioning enables you to explicitly control how rows map to partitions. You do this by specifying a list of discrete values for the partitioning column in the description for each partition. This is different from range partitioning, where a range of values is associated with a partition and with hash partitioning, where you have no control of the row-to-partition mapping. The advantage of list partitioning is that you can group and organize unordered and unrelated sets of data in a natural way.

```
CREATE TABLE sales_list
(salesman_id NUMBER(5), emp_name VARCHAR2(25), sales_area VARCHAR2(20),
sales_amount NUMBER(10), sales_date DATE) PARTITION BY LIST(sales_area)
(
PARTITION sales_south VALUES IN('Delhi', 'Mumbai','Kolkatta'),
PARTITION sales_north VALUES IN ('Bangalore', 'Chennai', 'Hyderabad'));
```

Composite Partitioning

Composite partitioning combines range and hash partitioning. Oracle first distributes data into partitions according to boundaries established by the partition ranges. Then Oracle uses a hashing algorithm to further divide the data into subpartitions within each range partition.

CREATE TABLE sales(s_productid NUMBER, s_saledate DATE, s_custid NUMBER, s_totalprice NUMBER) PARTITION BY RANGE (s_saledate) SUBPARTITION BY HASH (s_productid) SUBPARTITIONS 16

(PARTITION sal98q1 VALUES LESS THAN (TO_DATE('01-APR-1998', 'DD-MON-YYYY')),
PARTITION sal98q2 VALUES LESS THAN (TO_DATE('01-JUL-1998', 'DD-MON-YYYY')),
PARTITION sal98q3 VALUES LESS THAN (TO_DATE('01-OCT-1998', 'DD-MON-YYYY')),
PARTITION sal98q4 VALUES LESS THAN (TO_DATE('01-JAN-1999', 'DD-MON-YYYY')))

Index Partitioning

You can choose whether or not to inherit the partitioning strategy of the underlying tables. You can create both local and global indexes on a table partitioned by range, hash, or composite methods. Local indexes inherit the partitioning attributes of their related tables. For example, if you create a local index on a composite table, Oracle automatically partitions the local index using the composite method.

Exercise

1. Why we need partition? Explain.
2. Explain different types of partition with suitable examples.
3. Write a short note on RAID technology.

CHAPTER 9

DATA MART AND META DATA

9.1 INTRODUCTION

A data warehouse is a relational/multidimensional database that is designed for query and analysis rather than transaction processing. A data warehouse usually contains historical data that is derived from transaction data. It separates analysis workload from transaction workload and enables a business to consolidate data from several sources.

In addition to a relational/multidimensional database, a data warehouse environment often consists of an ETL solution, an OLAP engine, client analysis tools, and other applications that manage the process of gathering data and delivering it to business users.

There are three types of data warehouses:

1. **Enterprise Data Warehouse** - An enterprise data warehouse provides a central database for decision support throughout the enterprise.
2. **ODS (Operational Data Store)** - This has a broad enterprise wide scope, but unlike the real entertprise data warehouse, data is refreshed in near real time and used for routine business activity.
3. **Data Mart** - Datamart is a subset of data warehouse and it supports a particular region, business unit or business function.

Data warehouses and data marts are built on dimensional data modeling where fact tables are connected with dimension tables. This is most useful for users to access data since a database can be visualized as a cube of several dimensions. A data warehouse provides an opportunity for slicing and dicing that cube along each of its dimensions.

9.2 DATA MART

A data warehouse is a cohesive data model that defines the central data repository for an organization. A data mart is a data repository for a specific user group. It contains summarized data that the user group can easily understand, process, and apply. A data mart cannot stand alone; it requires a data warehouse. Because each data warehousing effort is unique, your company's data warehousing environment may differ slightly from what we are about to introduce.

Each data mart is a collection of tables organized according to the particular requirements of a user or group of users. Retrieving a collection of different kinds of data from a "normalized" warehouse can be complex and time-consuming. Hence the need to rearrange the data so they can be retrieved more easily. The notion of a "mart" suggests that it is organized for the ultimate consumers — with the potato chips, and video tapes all next to each other.

This organization does not have to follow any particular inherent rules or structures. Indeed, it may not even make sense. And however the marts are organized initially, the requirements are almost certain to change once the user has seen the implications of the request.

This means that the creation of data marts requires:

- ✧ Understanding of the business involved.
- ✧ Responsiveness to the user's stated objectives.
- ✧ Sufficient facility with database modeling and design to produce new tables quickly.
- ✧ Tools to convert models into data marts quickly.

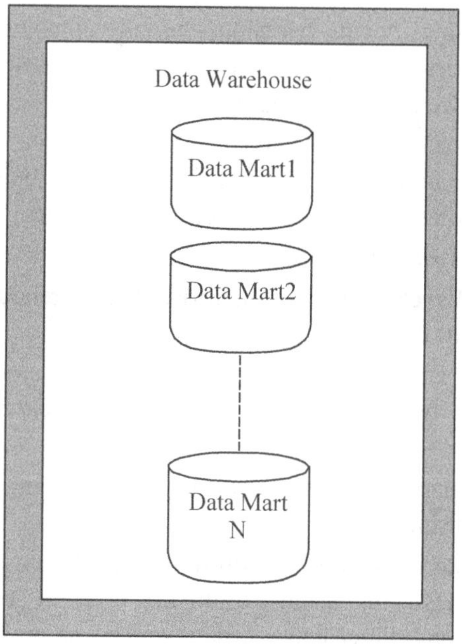

Fig. 9.1 Data warehouse and data marts

9.3 META DATA

For Example: In order to store data, over the years, many application designers in each branch have made their individual decisions as to how an application and database should be built. So source systems will be different in naming conventions, variable measurements, encoding structures, and physical attributes of data. Consider a bank that has got several branches in several countries, has millions of customers and the lines of business of the enterprise are savings, and loans. The following example explains how the data is integrated from source systems to target systems.

Example of Source Data

System name	*Attribute name*	*Column name*	*Datatype*	*Values*
Source System 1	Customer Application Date	CUSTOMER_ APPLICATION_DATE	NUMERIC (8, 0)	11012005
Source System 2	Customer Application Date	CUST_APPLICATION_ DATE	DATE	11012005
Source System 3	Application Date	APPLICATION_DATE	DATE	01NOV2005

In the aforementioned example, attribute name, column name, datatype and values are entirely different from one source system to another. This inconsistency in data can be avoided by integrating the data into a data warehouse with good standards.

Example of Target Data (Data Warehouse)

Target system	*Attribute name*	*Column name*	*Datatype*	*Values*
Record #1	Customer Application Date	CUSTOMER_ APPLICATION_DATE	DATE	01112005
Record #2	Customer Application Date	CUSTOMER_ APPLICATION_DATE	DATE	01112005
Record #3	Customer Application Date	CUSTOMER_ APPLICATION_DATE	DATE	01112005

In the above example of target data, attribute names, column names, and datatypes are consistent throughout the target system. This is how data from various source systems is integrated and accurately stored into the data warehouse.

Meta data is literally "data about data". It describes the kind of information in the warehouse, where it stored, how it relates to other information, where it comes from, and how it is related to the business. The topic of standardizing meta data across various products and applying a systems engineering approach to this process in order to facilitate data warehouse design is what this project intend to address.

A data warehouse stores current and historical data from disparate operational systems (*i.e.*, transactional databases) into one consolidated system where data is cleansed and restructured to support data analysis. We intend to create a design process for creating a data warehouse through the development of a metadata system. The meta data system we intend to create will provide a framework to organize and design the data warehouse. Using a systems engineering approach, this process will be used initially to help define the data warehouse requirements and it will then be used iteratively during the life of the data warehouse to update and integrate new dimensions of the warehouse.

In order to be effective, the user of the data warehouse must have access to meta data that is accurate and up to date. Without a good source of meta data to operate from, the job of the analyst is much more difficult and the work required for analysis is compounded significantly.

Understanding the role of the enterprise data model relative to the data warehouse is critical to a successful design and implementation of a data warehouse and its meta data management. Some specific challenges which involve the physical design tradeoffs of a data warehouse include:

- Granularity of data - refers to the level of detail held in the unit of data
- Partitioning of data - refers to the breakup of data into separate physical units that can be handled independently.
- Performance issues
- Data structures inside the warehouse
- Migration

For years, data has aggregated in the corporate world as a by-product of transaction processing and other uses of the computer. For the most part, the data that has accumulated has served only the immediate set of requirements for which is was initially intended. The data warehouse presents an alternative in data processing that represents the integrated information requirements of the enterprise. It is designed to support analytical processing for the entire business organization. Analytical processing looks across either various pieces of or the entire enterprise and identifies trends and patterns otherwise not apparent. These trends and patterns are absolutely vital to the vision of management in directing the organization.

Meta data itself is arguably the most critical element in effective data management. Effective tools must be used to properly store and use the meta data generated by the various systems.

9.3.1 Data Transformation and Load

Meta data may be used during transformation and load to describe the source data and any changes that need to be made. Whether or not you need to store any meta data for this process will depend on the complexity of the transformations that are to be applied to the data, when moving it from source to data warehouse. It will also depend on the number of source systems and the type of each system.

For each source data field the following information is required:

Source field

Unique identifier, name, type, location (system, object).

A unique identifier is required to avoid any confusion occurring between two fields of the same name from different sources. *Name, type, location* describe where the data comes from. *Name* is its local field name. *Type* is the storage type of data. *Location* is both the system comes from and the *object* contains it.

The destination field needs to be described in a similar way to the source.

Destination

Unique identifier, name, type, table name.

A unique identifier is needed to help avoid any confusion between commonly used field names. *Name* is the designation that the field will have in the base data within the data warehouse. Base data is used to distinguish between the original data load destination and any copies. Destination *type* is the database data type, such as clear, varchar, number. *Table name* is the name of the table field will be part of.

Transformation needs to be applied to turn the source data into the destination data.

Transformation(s)

Name, language (module name, syntax).

Name is a unique identifier that differentiates this from any other similar transformations. *Language* attribute contains the name of the language that the transformation written in. The other attributes are *module name* and *syntax*.

9.3.2 Data Management

Meta data is required to describe the data as it resides in the data warehouse. This is needed by the warehouse manager to allow it to track and control all data movements. Every object in the database needs to be described. Meta data is needed for all of the following:

Table

Columns (name, type)

Indexes

Columns (name, type)

Views

Columns (name, type)

Constraints

Name, type, table (columns)

To this end we will need to store meta data like the following for each field.

Field

Unique identifier, field name, description.

For each table the following information needs to be stored.

Table

Table name, columns (column_name, reference identifier)

Aggregations are a special case of tables, and they require the following meta data to be stored.

Aggregation

Aggregation name, columns (column_name, reference identifier, aggregation).

The functions listed below are examples of aggregation functions:

Min, max, average, sum

Partitions are subsets of a table, but they also need the information on the partition key and the data range that resides in the partition.

Partition

Partition name, table name (range allowed, range contained, partition key(reference identifier))

9.4 LEGACY SYSTEMS

The task of documenting legacy systems and mapping their columns to those of the central data warehouse is the worst part of any data warehouse project. Moreover, the particular characteristics of the project vary, depending on the nature, technology, and sites of those systems. Essential Strategies, Inc. has extended Oracle's Designer/2000 product to allow for reverse engineering of legacy systems—specifically providing the facility for mapping each column of a legacy system to an attribute of the corporate data model. Combining this with the mapping of each column in a data mart to an attribute of the data model provides direct mapping of original data to the view of them seen by users.

EXERCISE

1. Define meta data.
2. What is data mart? Give example.
3. What is legacy system?
4. Explain data management in meta data.

CHAPTER 10

BACKUP AND RECOVERY OF THE DATA WAREHOUSE

10.1 INTRODUCTION

One of the most important part is backup and recovery in a data warehouse. If your data is precious to you, then treat it accordingly. Human errors, Hardware, Software, Network, Process, system failure and the other unfrozen disasters can make your work vanish into digital nothingness in no time. It make sense backup your data on a regular basis .If such failure affects the operation of a database system ,it is required to recover the data base and return to normal operation as quick as possible. There are utilities that can backup entire partitions along with the operating system and everything else.

10.2 TYPES OF BACKUP

The definitions below should help to clarify the issue. These definitions apply to the back up of the database.

Complete Backup—The entire database is backed up at the same time. This includes all database data files and the journal files.

Partial Backup—Any backup that is not complete.

Cold Backup—Backup that is taken while the database is completely shut down. In a multi-instance environment, all instances of that database must be shut down.

Hot Backup—Any backup that is not cold is considered to be hot. The terminology comes from the fact that the database engine is up and running hence hot. There are special requirements that need to be observed if the hot backup is to be valid. These will vary from RDBMS to RDBMS.

Consider how these important issues affect backup plan:

- ✧ Realize that the restore is almost more important than the backup
- ✧ Create a hot backup
- ✧ Move your backup offline
- ✧ Perfect the connection between your production and backup servers
- ✧ Consider a warm backup
- ✧ Always reassess the situation

10.3 BACKUP THE DATA WAREHOUSE

Oracle RDBMS is basically a collection of physical database files. Backup and recovery problems are most likely to occur at this level. Three types of files must be backed up: database files, control files, and online redo log files. If you omit any of these files, you have not made a successful backup of the database.

Cold backups shut down the database. Hot backups take backups while the database is functioning. There are also supplemental backup methods, such as exports. Each type of backup has its advantages and disadvantages. The major types of instance recovery are cold restore, full database recovery, time-based recovery, and cancel-based recovery.

Oracle provides a server-managed infrastructure for backup, restore, and recovery tasks that enables simpler, safer operations at terabyte scale. Some of the highlights are:

- Details related to backup, restore, and recovery operations are maintained by the server in a recovery catalog and automatically used as part of these operations. This reduces administrative burden and minimizes the possibility of human errors.
- Backup and recovery operations are fully integrated with partitioning. Individual partitions, when placed in their own tablespaces, can be backed up and restored independently of the other partitions of a table.
- Oracle includes support for incremental backup and recovery, enabling operations to be completed efficiently within times proportional to the amount of changes, rather than the overall size of the database.
- The backup and recovery technology is highly scalable, and provides tight interfaces to industry-leading media management subsystems. This provides for efficient operations that can scale up to handle very large volumes of data. Open platforms for more hardware options & enterprise-level platforms.

Putting in place a backup and recovery plan for data warehouses is imperative. Even though most of the data comes from operational systems originally, you cannot always rebuild data warehouses in the event of a media failure (or a disaster). As operational data ages, it is removed from the operational databases, but it may still exist in the data warehouse. Furthermore, data warehouses often contain external data that, if lost, may have to be purchased.

We allow you to back up any number of computers to your account. You only pay a small one time fee for each additional computer. All computers will share the common pool of storage space.

Keeping a local backup allows you to save data way in excess of the storage that you purchase for online backup. For other backup products designed for local backup.

10.3.1 Create a Hot Backup

The best solution for critical systems is always to restore the backup once it has been made onto another machine. This will also provide you with a "hot" backup that is ready to be used, should your production database ever crash. If you can't afford this higher cost, you should at least do periodic test restores.

10.3.2 Consider a Warm (Not Hot) Backup

After you install hot backups and build a solid network, can you relax? Sort of, except there's one thing you still need to worry about.

Hot backups are great because they are extremely current. The minute data is changed on the primary server, you propagate that change to your backup server.

But that very same close binding also comes with its own dangers. Consider what happens if someone accidentally deletes the wrong data. For example, say an administrator accidentally drops the accounts table in the database. (I'm not making this up; this actually happened at a client of mine.) The inadvertent deletion will immediately get propagated to the backup, too.

If every second of downtime is expensive, you should consider creating a copy of the database that is kept "warm"—*i.e.*, fairly recent but not as recent as your hot backup. For example, you might set the hot backup within a minute of the primary server, but deliberately keep your warm backup 30 minutes behind your primary. That way, you only have to restore the last several transaction logs rather than start from scratch.

10.3.3 Tape Backup Storage

- ✧ Tape backup of customers' data on SAN
- ✧ Tape backup of Veritas disk storage
- ✧ Tape backup of customers' data direct from network
- ✧ Tape archiving
- ✧ Off-site tape storage

10.3.4 What is SureWest Broadband's Online Backup Service?

It is Internet-based services that allows computer users to routinely backup and recover their data using a secure connection and safely store it in the SureWest Broadband Data Storage Warehouse until it is needed.

If you use your computer for business or personal use, you need to always have a backup of your data files in the event of software, hardware or human error. Ideally you should keep a copy of this data at some location other than your home or place of business. If your house burns down and your backups are sitting on the shelf next to your computer, they too will be lost.

You need to make backups of your important data to prevent a total loss in the event of any kind of system failure or human error. Simple data backup can be done by saving your data to multiple locations, copying the data from its original location to removable media, another hard drive, or another computer's hard drive on the network.

You also need to have multiple versions of your information backed up. If you are working on a spreadsheet over a period of several days, it's best to keep a snapshot of every day's work. This is easily done with an online backup service.

To make this task easier, SureWest Broadband has licensed Backup Software from NovaStor, a leader in the backup business, to enable users to make backup copies of their data. Most users do not want to be bothered with managing the tasks necessary for maintaining their own backups, so a new type of backup system was needed. It's known as online backup.

Online backup software is designed to routinely copy your important files to a private, secure location on the Internet by transmitting your data over your existing Internet connection. All of your data is encrypted before it is sent to our storage network to protect your privacy. If you have a working Internet connection on your computer, you can use SureWest Broadband's Online Backup Service to keep your important files safe from disaster on a daily basis.

10.3.5 What is a FastBIT Backup?

The FastBIT patching process is the core technology behind NovaStor's speedy backup program. The patching process involves the comparison of two different versions of the same file and extracting the differences between the files. When the differences are extracted from the two files, they are saved into a new file and compressed into what is known as a patch. The patch file is often 85% to 1010.10% smaller than the file which the patch was extracted from originally.

10.4 DATA WAREHOUSE RECOVERY MODELS

The model chosen can have a dramatic impact on performance, especially during data loads. There are three recovery models: full, bulk-logged, and simple. The recovery model of a new database is inherited from the model database when the new database is created. The model for a database can be changed after the database has been created.

- Full recovery provides the most flexibility for recovering databases to an earlier point in time.
- Bulk-logged recovery provides higher performance and lower log space consumption for certain large-scale operations (for example, create index or bulk copy). It does this at the expense of some flexibility of point-in-time recovery.
- Simple recovery provides the highest performance and lowest log space consumption, but it does so with significant exposure to data loss in the event of a system failure. When using the simple recovery model, data is recoverable only to the last (most recent) full database or differential backup. Transaction log backups are not usable for recovering transactions because, in this model, the transactions are truncated from the log upon checkpoint. This creates the potential for data loss. After the log space is no longer needed for recovery from server failure (active transactions), it is truncated and reused.

Knowledgeable administrators can use this recovery model feature to significantly speed up data loads and bulk operations. However, the amount of exposure to data loss varies with the model chosen. It is imperative that the risks be thoroughly understood before choosing a recovery model.

Each recovery model addresses a different need. Trade-offs are made depending on the model you chose. The trade-offs that occur pertain to performance, space utilization (disk or tape), and protection against data loss. When you choose a recovery model, you are deciding among the following business requirements:

- Performance of large-scale operations (for example, index creation or bulk loads)
- Data loss exposure (for example, the loss of committed transactions)

✧ Transaction log space consumption

✧ Simplicity of backup and recovery procedures

Depending on what operations you are performing, one model may be more appropriate than another. Before choosing a recovery model, consider the impact it will have. The following table provides helpful information.

Recovery model	*Benefits*	*Work loss exposure*	*Recover to point in time?*
Simple	Permits high-performance bulk copy operations. Reclaims log space to keep space requirements small.	Changes since the most recent database or differential backup must be redone	Can recover to the end of any backup. Then changes must be redone.
Full	No work is lost due to a lost or damaged data file. Can recover to an arbitrary point in time (for example, prior to application or user error).	Normally none. If the log is damaged, changes since the most recent log backup must be redone.	Can recover to any point in time.
Bulk-Logged	Permits high-performance bulk copy operations. Minimal log space is used by bulk operations.	If the log is damaged, or bulk operations occurred since the most recent log backup, changes since that last backup must be redone. Otherwise, no work is lost.	Can recover to the end of any backup. Then changes must be redone.

EXERCISE

1. How will you backup the data warehouse? Explain.
2. What are the types of backup?
3. Explain data warehouse recovery model.

CHAPTER 11

PERFORMANCE TUNING AND FUTURE OF DATA WAREHOUSE

11.1 INTRODUCTION

A well planned methodology is the key to success in performance tuning. Different tuning strategies vary in their effectiveness. Furthermore, systems with different purposes, such as online transaction processing systems and decision support systems, likely require different tuning methods.

11.2 PRIORITIZED TUNING STEPS

The following steps provide a recommended method for tuning an Oracle database. These steps are prioritized in order of diminishing returns: steps with the greatest effect on performance appear first. For optimal results, therefore, resolve tuning issues in the order listed: from the design and development phases through instance tuning.

Step 1: Tune the Business Rules

Step 2: Tune the Data Design

Step 3: Tune the Application Design

Step 4: Tune the Logical Structure of the Database

Step 5: Tune Database Operations

Step 6: Tune the Access Paths

Step 7: Tune Memory Allocation

Step 8: Tune I/O and Physical Structure

Step 9: Tune Resource Contention

Step 10: Tune the Underlying Platform(s)

After completing these steps, reassess your database performance and decide whether further tuning is necessary.

Tuning is an iterative process. Performance gains made in later steps may pave the way for further improvements in earlier steps, so additional passes through the tuning process may be useful. Fig. 11.1 illustrates the tuning method:

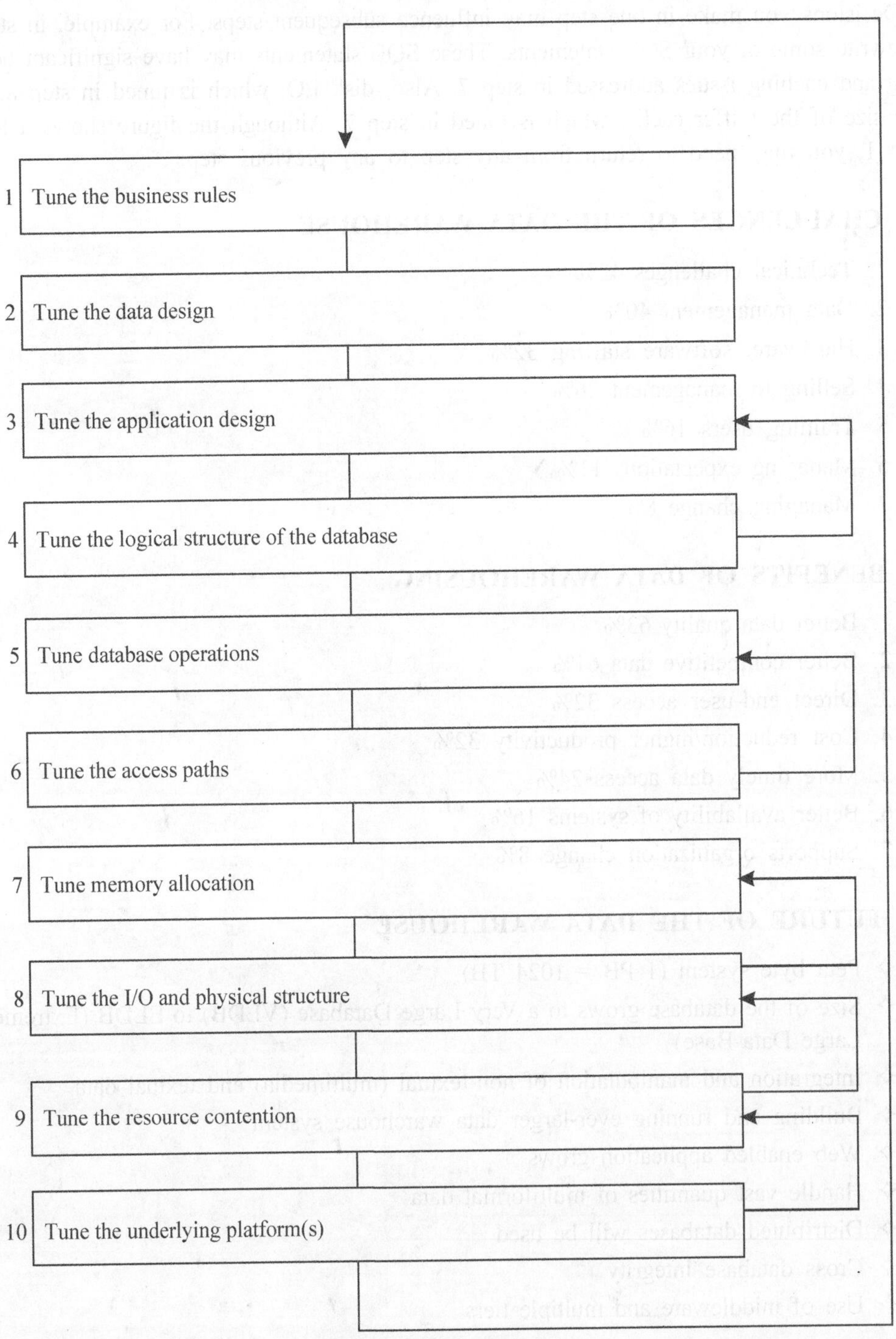

Fig. 11.1. The tuning method

Decisions you make in one step may influence subsequent steps. For example, in step 5 you may rewrite some of your SQL statements. These SQL statements may have significant bearing on parsing and caching issues addressed in step 7. Also, disk I/O, which is tuned in step 8, depends on the size of the buffer cache, which is tuned in step 7. Although the figure shows a loop back to step 1, you may need to return from any step to any previous step.

11.3 CHALLENGES OF THE DATA WAREHOUSE

1. Technical challenges 42%
2. Data management 40%
3. Hardware, software staffing 32%
4. Selling to management 26%
5. Training users 16%
6. Managing expectations 11%
7. Managing change 8%

11.4 BENEFITS OF DATA WAREHOUSING

1. Better data quality 63%
2. Better competitive data 61%
3. Direct end-user access 32%
4. Cost reduction/higher productivity 32%
5. More timely data access 24%
6. Better availability of systems 16%
7. Supports organization change 8%

11.5 FUTURE OF THE DATA WAREHOUSE

- Peta byte system (1 PB = 1024 TB)
- Size of the database grows to a Very Large Database (VLDB) to ELDB (Extremely Very Large Data Base)
- Integration and manipulation of non-textual (multimedia) and textual data
- Building and running ever-larger data warehouse system
- Web enabled application grows
- Handle vast quantities of multiformat data
- Distributed databases will be used
- Cross database integrity
- Use of middleware and multiple tiers

11.6 NEW ARCHITECTURE OF DATA WAREHOUSE

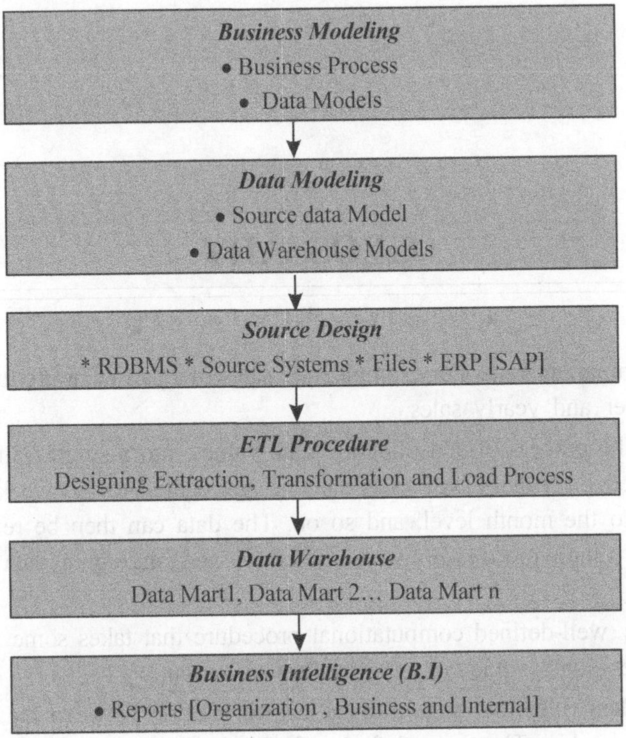

Fig. 11.2 Data warehouse architecture diagram

EXERCISE

1. Explain tuning the data warehouse.
2. Draw the architecture diagram of data warehouse.
3. What is the future scope of data warehouse?

GLOSSARY

Aggregate: Summarized data. For example, unit sales of a particular product could be aggregated by day, month, quarter and yearly sales.

Aggregation: The process of consolidating data values into a single value. For example, sales data could be collected on a daily basis and then be aggregated to the week level, the week data could be aggregated to the month level, and so on. The data can then be referred to as aggregate data. Aggregation is synonymous with summarization, and aggregate data is synonymous with summary data.

Algorithm: Any well-defined computational procedure that takes some value or set of values as input, and produces some value or set of values as output.

Association Rules: rules that state a statistical correlation between the occurrence of certain attributes in a database table. The general form of an association rule is X1, X2,....Xn =>y. This means that the attributes X1, X2,....Xn predict Y.

Attribute: A descriptive characteristic of one or more levels. Attributes represent logical groupings that enable end users to select data based on like characteristics. In RDBMS, an attribute is a column in a dimension that characterizes elements of a single level.

Business Intelligence Tools: Software that enables business users to see and use large amounts of complex data.

Bit(s): acronym for binary digit. A unit of computer storage that can store 2 values, 0 or 1.

Byte: A standard unit of storage. A byte consists of 8 bits. Basically, a byte is a sufficient to store a single character.

Classification: A subdivision of a set of examples into a number of classes.

Cleansing: The process of resolving inconsistencies and fixing the anomalies in source data, typically as part of the ETL process. See also ETL.

Clickstream Data: Data regarding web browsing

Cluster: A tightly coupled group of SMP machines, with the database is shut down.

Coding: Operations on a database to transform or simplify data in order to prepare it for a machine-learning algorithm.

Cold Backup: A database backup taken while the database is shut down.

Common Warehouse Meta Data (CWM): A repository standard used by Oracle data warehousing, decision support, and OLAP tools including Oracle Warehouse Builder. The CWM repository schema is a standalone product that other products can share each product owns only the objects within the CWM repository that it creates.

Confidence: Given the association rule X1, X2...Xn=>Y, the confidence is the percentage of records for which Y holds, within the group of records for which X1, X2,...Xn holds.

Data: Any symbolic representation of facts or ideas from which information can potentially be extracted.

Data Selection: The stage of selecting the right data for a KDD process.

Data Source: A database, application, repository, or file that contributes data to a warehouse.

Data Mart: A data warehouse that is designed for a particular line of business, such as sales, marketing, or finance. In a dependent data mart, the data can be derived from an enterprise-wide data warehouse. In an independent data mart, data can be collected directly from sources. See also data warehouse.

Data Mining: The actual discovery phase of a knowledge discovery process.

Data Warehouse: A relational database that is designed for query and analysis rather than transaction processing. A data warehouse usually contains historical data that is derived from transaction data, but it can include data from other sources. It separates analysis workload from transaction workload and enables a business to consolidate data from several sources. In addition to a relational database, a data warehouse environment often consists of an ETL solution, an OLAP engine, client analysis tools, and other applications that manage the process of gathering data and delivering it to business users. See also ETL, OLAP.

Denormalize: The process of allowing redundancy in a table so that it can remain flat. Contrast with normalize.

Derived Fact (or Measure): A fact (or measure) that is generated from existing data using a mathematical operation or a data transformation. Examples include averages, totals, percentages, and differences.

Decision Trees: A decision tree consists of nodes and branches, starting from a single root node. Each node represents a test or decision. Depending on the outcome of the decision, one chooses a certain branch and when a terminal node(or leaf) is reached a decision on a class assignment is made.

Deep Knowledge: Knowledge that is hidden within a database and can only be recovered if one is given certain clues.

Dimension: A structure, often composed of one or more hierarchies, that categorizes data. Several distinct dimensions, combined with measures, enable end users to answer business questions. Commonly used dimensions are customer, product, and time.

Dimension Data: Data stored externally to the fact data, which contains expanded information on specific dimensions of the fact data.

Dimension Table: Part of star schema. A table which holds dimension data.

Drill: To navigate from one item to a set of related items. Drilling typically involves navigating up and down through the levels in a hierarchy. When selecting data, you can expand or collapse a hierarchy by drilling down or up in it, respectively. See also drill down, drill up.

Drill Down: To expand the view to include child values that are associated with parent values in the hierarchy. (See also drill, drill up)

Drill Up: To collapse the list of descendant values that are associated with a parent value in the hierarchy.

Enrichment: A stage of the KDD process in which new data is added to the existing selection.

Element: An object or process. For example, a dimension is an object, a mapping is a process, and both are elements.

ETL: Extraction, transformation, and loading. ETL refers to the methods involved in accessing and manipulating source data and loading it into a data warehouse. The order in which these processes are performed varies. Note that ETT (extraction, transformation, transportation) and E T M (extraction, transformation, move) are sometimes used instead of ETL. (See also data warehouse, extraction, transportation)

Extraction: The process of taking data out of a source as part of an initial phase of ETL

Fact Data: The fact data is the basic core data that will be stored in the data warehouse. It is called fact data because it will correspond to business-related facts such as call record data for a telco, or account transaction data for a bank.

Fact Table: Part of a star schema. The central table that contains the fact data.

File System: An area of space set aside to contain files. The file system will contain a root directory in which other directories or files can be created.

File-to-table Mapping: Maps data from flat files to tables in the warehouse.

Genetic Algorithm: A class of machine-learning algorithm that is based on the theory of evaluation.

Granularity: The level of detail of the facts stored in a data warehouse.

Hidden Knowledge: Knowledge that is hidden in a database and that cannot be recovered by a simple SQL query. More advanced machine-learning techniques involving many different SQL queries are necessary to find hidden knowledge.

Hierarchy: A logical structure that uses ordered levels as a means of organizing data. A hierarchy can be used to define data aggregation; for example, in a Time dimension, a hierarchy might be used to aggregate data from the month level to the quarter level to the year level. A hierarchy can also be used to define a navigational drill path, regardless of whether the levels in the hierarchy represent aggregated totals.

Inductive Learning: Learning by generalizing form examples.

Information: Meaningful data.

KDD: Knowledge Discovery in Databases: The non-trivial extraction of implicit, previously unknown and potentially useful information from data.

Knowledge: A collection of interesting and useful patterns in a database.

Learning: An individual learns how to carry out a certain task by making a transition from a situation in which the task cannot be carried out to a situation in which the same task can be carried out under the same circumstances.

Machine Learning: A sub-discipline of computer science that deals with the design and implementation of learning algorithms.

Materialized View: A pre-computed table comprising aggregated and/or joined data from fact and possibly dimension tables. Also known as a summary or aggregate table.

Meta Data: Data about data. Meta data is data that describes the source, location and meaning of another piece of data. For example, the schema design of a data warehouse is typically stored in a repository as metadata, which is used to generate scripts used to build and populate the data warehouse. A repository contains meta data. Examples include: for data, the definition of a source to target transformation that is used to generate and populate the data warehouse; for information, definitions of tables, columns and associations that are stored inside a relational modeling tool; for business rules, discount by 10 percent after selling 1,000 items.

Multi-dimensional Knowledge: A table with n independent attributes can be seen as an n-dimensional space. Some regularities represented in such a table cannot easily be detected when the table has a standard two-dimensional representation. WE have to explore the relationship

Neural Networks: A class of learning algorithm consisting of multiple nodes that communicate through their connecting synapses. Neural networks initiate the structure of biological nervous systems.

Normalize: In a relational database, the process of removing redundancy in data by separating the data into multiple tables. Contrast with denormalize.

Operational Data Store (ODS): The cleaned, transformed data from a particular source database.

OLAP: Online analytical Processing

OLTP: Online transaction processing. An OLTP system is designed to handle a large volume of small predefined transactions.

Online Backup: A database backup taken while the database is open and potentially in use. The RDBMS will need to have special facilities to ensure that data in the backup is consistent.

Overnight Processing: Any processing that needs to be done to accomplish the daily loading, cleaning, aggregation, maintenance and backup of data, in order to make that new data available to the users for the following day.

Patterns: Structures in a database that are statistically relevant.

Prediction: The result of the application of a theory or a rule in a specific case.

Query Tools: Tools designed to query a database.

Shallow Knowledge: The information stored in a database that can be retrieved with a single query.

Snowflake Schema: A variant of the star schema where each dimension can have its own dimensions.

Star Schema: A logical structure that has a fact table in the centre with dimension table radiating off of this central table. The fact table will generally be extremely large in comparison to its dimension tables. There will be a foreign key in the fact table for each dimension table.

Star Flake Schema: This is a hybrid structure that contains a mix of star and snowflake schemas. Some dimensions may be represented in both forms to cater different query requirements.

Statistical Techniques: Techniques used in statistics.

Supervised Algorithms: Algorithms that need the control of a human operator during their execution.

Support: Given the association rule X1, X2,...Xn => Y, the support is the percentage of records for which X1....Xn and Y both hold.

Transportation: The process of moving copied or transformed data from a source to a data warehouse.

Unsupervised Algorithms: The opposite of supervised algorithms.

Validation: The process of verifying metadata definitions and configuration parameters.

Versioning : The ability to create new versions of a data warehouse project for new requirements and changes.

Verification: The validation of a theory on the basis of a finite number of examples.

Visualization Techniques: A class of graphic techniques used to visualize the contents of a database.

MULTIPLE-CHOICE QUESTIONS

1. **A data warehouse is a.........collection of data in support of management's decision-making process.**
   (a) Integrated and subject oriented
   (b) Time variant
   (c) Non volatile
   (d) All the above
2. **Who is the originator of the data warehousing concept?**
   (a) Johan McIntyre
   (b) Bill Inmon
   (c) Bill Gates
   (d) Chris Erickson
3. **Data which is not updated or changed in any way once they enter the data warehouse are called:**
   (a) Non-volatile
   (b) Integrated
   (c) Cluster
   (d) Coding
4. **Data cleansing**
   (a) The process of resolving inconsistencies and fixing the anomalies in source data,
   (b) Removes duplication
   (c) Reconciles differences between various styles of data collection
   (d) All the above
5. **SMP means**
   (a) Systematic multi-processing
   (b) Stage multi-processing
   (c) Symmetric multi-processing
   (d) None of the above

6. **OLTP means**
   (a) Off line transaction processing
   (b) Off line transaction product
   (c) On line transaction product
   (d) On line transaction processing
7. **Data we use to run our business is**
   (a) Historical data
   (b) Operational data
   (c) Statistical data
   (d) Transactional data
8. **Data marts are .... which are small in size.**
   (a) Business houses
   (b) Workgroups or departmental warehouses
   (c) Data structures
   (d) Company warehouses
9. **OLAP means**
   (a) Off line adaptive processing
   (b) Off line adaptive product
   (c) On line adaptive product
   (d) On line analytical processing
10. **Composite partitioning combines .... and .... partitioning.**
   (a) Range & hash
   (b) Hash & index
   (c) Index and range
   (d) None of the above

Answer

1 (d); 2 (b); 3 (a); 4 (a); 5 (c); 6 (d); 7 (b); 8 (b); 9 (d); 10 (a).

FREQUENTLY ASKED QUESTIONS AND ANSWERS

1. What is a data warehouse?

A data warehouse is the "corporate memory". It is a subject oriented, point-in-time, inquiry only collection of operational data. Typical relational databases are designed for on-line transactional processing (OLTP) and do not meet the requirements for effective on-line analytical processing (OLAP). As a result, data warehouses are designed differently than traditional relational databases.

2. What is ETL/How does Oracle support the ETL process?

ETL is the Data Warehouse acquisition processes of extracting, transforming (or transporting) and loading (ETL) data from source systems into the data warehouse.

Oracle supports the ETL process with their "Oracle Warehouse Builder" product. Many new features in the Oracle9i database will also make ETL processing easier. For example: New MERGE command (also called UPSERT, Insert and update information in one step); External Tables allows users to run SELECT statements on external data files (with pipelining support).

3. What is the difference between a data warehouse and a data mart?

There are inherent similarities between the basic constructs used to design a data warehouse and a data mart. In general a Data Warehouse is used on an enterprise level, while Data Marts is used on a business division/department level. A data mart only contains the required subject specific data for local analysis.

What is the difference between a W/H and an OLTP application?

Typical relational databases are designed for on-line transactional processing (OLTP) and do not meet the requirements for effective on-line analytical processing (OLAP). As a result, data warehouses are designed differently than traditional relational databases.

Warehouses are time referenced, subject-oriented, non-volatile (read only) and integrated. OLTP databases are designed to maintain atomicity, consistency and integrity (the "ACID" tests). Since a data warehouse is not updated, these constraints are relaxed.

4. What is the difference between OLAP, ROLAP, MOLAP and HOLAP?

ROLAP, MOLAP and HOLAP are specialized OLAP (Online Analytical Processing) applications. ROLAP stands for Relational OLAP. Users see their data organized in cubes with dimensions, but the data is really stored in a Relational Database (RDBMS) like Oracle. The RDBMS will store data at a fine grain level, response times are usually slow.

MOLAP stands for Multidimensional OLAP. Users see their data organized in cubes with dimensions, but the data is store in a Multi-dimensional database (MDBMS) like Oracle Express Server. In a MOLAP system lot of queries have a finite answer and performance is usually critical and fast.

HOLAP stands for Hybrid OLAP, it is a combination of both worlds. Seagate Software's Holos is an example HOLAP environment. In a HOLAP system one will find queries on aggregated data as well as on detailed data.

5. **What is the difference between an ODS and a W/H?**

An ODS (operational data store) is an integrated database of operational data. Its sources include legacy systems and it contains current or near term data. An ODS may contain 30 to 90 days of information. A warehouse typically contains years of data (time referenced). Data warehouses group data by subject ather than by activity (subject-oriented). Other properties are: Non-volatile (read only) and Integrated.

6. **What Oracle tools can be used to design and build a W/H?**

Data Warehouse Builder (or Oracle data mart builder), Oracle designer, Oracle express, Express objects.

7. **When should one use an MD-database (multi-dimensional database) and not a relational one?**

Data in a multi-dimensional database is stored as business people views it, allowing them to slice and dice the data to answer business questions. When designed correctly, an OLAP database will provide must faster response times for analytical queries. Normal relational databases store data in two-dimensional tables and analytical queries against them are normally very slow.

8. **What is a star schema? Why does one design this way? Why?**

A single "fact table" containing a compound primary key, with one segment for each "dimension," and additional columns of additive, numeric facts. It allows for the highest level of flexibility of metadata Low maintenance as the data warehouse matures Best possible performance.

9. **When should you use a STAR and when a SNOW-FLAKE schema?**

The star schema is the simplest data warehouse schema. Snow flake schema is similar to the star schema. It normalizes dimension table to save data storage space. It can be used to represent hierarchies of information.

10. **What is the difference between Oracle express and Oracle discoverer?**

Express is an MD database and development environment. Discoverer is an ad-hoc end-user query tool.

11. **How can Oracle materialized views be used to speed up data warehouse queries?**

With "Query rewrite" (QUERY_REWRITE_ENABLED=TRUE in INIT.ORA) Oracle can direct queries to use pre-aggregated tables instead of scanning large tables to answer complex queries. Materialized views in a W/H environments is typically referred to as summaries, because they store summarized data.

12. What Oracle features can be used to optimize the warehouse system?

From Oracle8*i* One can transport tablespaces between Oracle databases. Using this feature one can easily "detach" a tablespace for archiving purposes. One can also use this feature to quickly move data from an OLTP database to a warehouse database. Data partitioning allows one to split big tables into smaller more manageable sub-tables (partitions). Data is automatically directed to the correct partition based on data ranges or hash values. Oracle materialized views can be used to pre-aggregate data. The query optimizer can direct queries to summary/ roll-up tables instead of the detail data tables (query rewrite). This will dramatically speed-up warehouse queries and saves valuable machine resources. Oracle parallel query can be used to speed up data retrieval by using multiple processes (and CPUs) to process a single task.

13. What tools can be used to design and build a W/H?

ETL processing using informatica , OLAP processing using cognos, business objects, designing data W/H using ERWIN, ETL processing using Data stage 7.5, ETL processing using Oracle DataPump, exp/imp and SQL*LOADER.

14. What is granularity?

The first step in designing a fact table is to determine the **granularity** of the fact table. By **granularity**, we mean the lowest level of information that will be stored in the fact table. This constitutes two steps: Determine which dimensions will be included and determine where along the hierarchy of each dimension the information will be kept. The determining factors usually go back to the requirements.

15. What is drill down and drill up?

Drill down—To expand the view to include child values that are associated with parent values in the hierarchy drill up—To collapse the list of descendant values that are associated with a parent value in the hierarchy.

MODEL QUESTION PAPERS

MCA DEGREE EXAMINATIONS

Data mining

Time: 3 hrs $5 \times 15 = 75$

1. *a.* What do you mean by expanding universe of data?
   b. Explain the term "data mining"

(or)

2. *a.* Explain, what are the practical applications of data mining.
   b. Distinguish between data mining and query tools.
3. With a suitable diagram explain the architecture of data warehouse.

(or)

4. What are the challenges in creating and maintaining a data warehouse? Explain in detail with suitable example.
5. What is OLAP? Explain the various tools available for OLAP.

(or)

6. Write short notes on (i) K–nearest neighbour, (ii) Decision trees.
7. Explain the various steps involved in knowledge discovery process.

(or)

8. Write short notes on (i) Data selection, (ii) Data cleaning, (iii) Data enrichment.
9. Explain about data compression.

(or)

10. Explain the term denormalization.

MCA DEGREE EXAMINATIONS

Data mining

Time: 3 hrs $5 \times 15 = 75$

1. *a.* What is data mining and data warehousing?
   b. How computer system that can learn?
   c. Discuss data mining in marketing.

(or)

2. *a.* Explain the practical applications of data mining.
   b. Write an account on machine learning and methodology of science.
   c. How query language suits to data mining operation?
3. *a.* Write in detail about manufacturing machine.
   b. Write short notes on cost justification.

(or)

4. *a.* Give an account of the need for decision support-system for business and scientific applications.
5. Write in detail about the use of artificial neural network and genetic algorithm for data mining.

(or)

6. What are OLAP tools? Explain various tools available for OLAP.
7. What are the different kinds of knowledge? How to develop a knowledge discovery database project?

(or)

8. Explain the data selection, cleaning, enrichment, coding and analysis of knowledge discovery process.
9. What are the primitives of data mining? Explain the data mining primitives in SQL.

(or)

10. Explain the following terminologies:
    Learning as compression of data set,
    Information content of a message,
    Noise and redundancy,
    Fuzzy database,
    Relational databases.

MCA DEGREE EXAMINATIONS

Data mining

Time: 3 hrs $5 \times 15 = 75$

1. *a.* What is meant by data mining?
   b. Compare data mining with query tools.
   (or)
2. *a.* Explain the concept of learning.
   b. Explain the complexity of search space with an example of a kangaroo in mist.
3. What is data warehouse? Why do we need it? Explain briefly.
   (or)
4. Explain the difficulties of a client/server and data warehousing.
5. Explain the knowledge discovery process in detail.
   (or)
6. Write a note on neural networks.
7. a. Explain the goal of KDD.
   b. What are the ten golden rules for reliable data mining?
   (or)
8. Write short notes on (i) Data selection, (ii) Data cleaning, (iii) Data enrichment.
9. Explain briefly the reconstruction foreign key relationship with suitable example.
   (or)
10. Explain the following: (i) Denormalization, (ii) Data mining primitives.

B. Tech DEGREE EXAMINATIONS

Data mining and warehousing

Time: 3 hrs $5 \times 15 = 75$

1. What is meant by data mining?
   Compare data mining and query tools.
   Explain in detail about data mining in marketing.
   (or)
2. Explain in detail the knowledge discovery process.
3. Explain in detail about self learning computer systems and concept learning.
   (or)

4. Explain about visualization techniques and OLAP tools.
5. Discuss about system process architecture design and database schema.

(or)

6. Discuss about system and data warehouse process managers.
7. Explain in detail the physical layout security, backup and recovery.

(or)

8. Explain about service level agreement and operating the data warehouse.
9. Explain about capacity planning and tuning the data warehouse.

(or)

10. How do you test the data warehouse? Explain.

B. Tech DEGREE EXAMINATIONS

Data mining and warehousing

Time: 3 hrs $5 \times 15 = 75$

1. Define data mining? Write in detail about information and production factor.
2. Write in detail about data mining and query tools.
3. Explain in detail self learning computer systems.
4. Discuss in detail data mining and data warehouse.
5. Write in detail about data selection, cleaning, enrichment and coding.
6. Discuss in detail visualization techniques.
7. Write in detail about knowledge discover in database environment.
8. Write in detail about meta data and system and data warehouse process managers.
9. Discuss in detail about database design schema and partitioning strategy.
10. Explain in detail hardware architecture.
11. Explain backup and recovery.
12. Explain in detail hardware physical layout security.
13. Discuss how one can operate the data warehouse.
14. Explain in detail data warehouse features.
15. Explain how you can true and test the data warehouse.

B. Tech DEGREE EXAMINATIONS

Data mining and warehousing

Time: 3 hrs $5 \times 15 = 75$

1. *a.* With a neat sketch, explain the architecture of a data mining system.

   b. Explain with neat sketch, data mining as step in the process of knowledge discovery.

2. *a.* Data mining plays a role in self learning computer systems. With suitable examples and relevant description justify the above statement.

b. Differentiate between data mining and data warehousing.

3. What is market-basket analysis? Explain with an example.

   With relevant examples explain how association rules can be mined from large data sets.

4. Discuss with simple case studies the role of neural networks in data mining.

   What are decision trees? Discuss their applications.

5. Explain with relevant diagrams the steps involved in designing a database schema.

   What is meta data? Discuss with an example.

6. With a neat sketch explain the architecture of a data warehouse "A data warehouse contains subject oriented data". Justify the above statement.

7. List the basic hardware architecture for a data warehouse. Give the necessary description also.

   List the steps involved in operating the data warehouse.

8. With relevant examples discuss the need for backup and recovery with respect to a data warehouse.

   What are the different security issues in data warehousing?

9. What is data warehouse tuning? Discuss the need for data warehouse tuning, with related case studies.

10. Explain, in detail, the procedure and the need for testing the data warehouse.

BIBLIOGRAPHY

BOOKS

Fayyad U.M., Piatetsky-shapiro G., Smyth P. and Uthurusamy K. (Eds.) (1996) **Advance in Knowledge Discovery and Data Mining,** MIT Press, 1996.

Becker, S. et al. (1988) **Improving the Convergence of Back Propagation Learning with Second Order Methods,** MIT Press, 1988.

Hamilton J.D. (1994) **Time Series Analysis,** Princeton University Press, 1994.

Mozer, M.C. (1993) **Neural Net Architecture for Temporal Sequence Processing, Predicting Future and Understanding the Past** (Eds. A. Weigend and N. Gershenfeld), Addison Wesley Pub., 1993.

Kimball R., **The Data Warehouse Toolkit,** John Wiley & Sons, 1996.

Elmasri R., Navathe S. 1999, **Fundamental of Database Systems, Part I and Part II,** MIT Press, 1999.

Teutsch S.M., Churchill R.E. (Eds.), **Principles and Practice of Public Health Surveillance,** NY: Oxford University Press, 1994.

Brin S., Motwani R., Ullman J.D., Tsur S., **Dynamic Itemset Counting and Implications Rules for Market Basket Data,** In: ACM Press, 1994 .

Doebbeling N.B. **Epidemics: Identification and Management,** In: Wenzel RP (Ed), **Prevention and Control of Nosocomial Infections,** Baltimore, Md: Williams and Wilkins, 1993.

Jean-mare Adamo, **Data Mining for Association Rules and Sequential Patterns,** NY: Springer-Verlag, 2000.

T.W. Anderson, **Statistical Analysis of Time Series,** NY: John Wiley & Sons, 1971.

Peter J. Brockwell and Richard A. Davis, **Introduction to Time Series and Forecasting,** NY: Springer–Verlag ,1996.

Ramon C. Barquin & Herbert A. Edelstein, Eds, **Building, Using and Managing the Data Warehouse,** Englewood Cliffs, NJ: Prentice Hall PTR, 1997.

Cristopher M. Bishop, **Neural Networks for Pattern Recognition,** NY: Oxford University Press, 1995.

Margaret H. Dunhan, **Data Mining Introductory and Advanced Topics,** Pearson Education, 2004.

Han J., Kamber M., **Data Mining: Concepts and Techniques,** Morgan Kaufman, 2000.

Pieter Adriaans Dolf Zantinge, **Data Mining,** Addison Wesley, 2000.

Sam Anahory Dennis Murray, **Data Warehousing in the Real World,** Pearson Education, 2000.

Inman, **Data Warehouse Design.**

Paul Lane, et al. Oracle9*i*, **Data Warehousing Guide,** Release 1 (9.0.1) Oracle Corporation.

JOURNALS AND PUBLICATIONS

Radding, Alan, **Support Decision Makers with a Data Warehouse,** Datamation, Vol 41(5) March 15, 1995.

Appleton, Elaine, **The Right Server for Your Data Warehouse,** Datamation Vol 41(5) March 15, 1995.

Bustamente, G. G. & Sorenson, K., **Decision Support at Lands' End – An Evolution,** IBM System Journal, Vol 33(2), 1994.

Koslow, Phyllis and Inmon, Bill, **Commandeering Mainframe Database for Data Warehouse Use,** Application Development Trends, Vol 1(8), Aug. 1994.

Brachman, R.J., Khabaza, T., Kloesgen, W., Piatetsky-Shapiro, G., and Simoudis, E. (1996) **Mining Business Databases,** Communications of the ACM, Vol. 39, No. 11, November, 1996.

Murata, Noboru et al. (1991), **Artificial Neural Networks**

Soulie, Francois (1991), **Artificial Neural Networks**, Vol. 1, 605–615.

WEBSITES

http://cs.felk.cvut.cz/~xobitko/ga/

http://www.generation5.org/aisolutions/ga_tsp.shtm

http://www.doc.ic.ac.uk/~nd/surprise_96/journal/vol4/tcw2/report.htm

http://www.olapcouncil.org

http://www.arborsoft.com/OLAP.html.

http://pwp.starnetinc.com/larryg/articles.html

http://www-east.elsevier.com/ida/browse/96-1/ida96-1.htm.

http://www.ncbi.nlm.nih.gov.uk/complications/ESRD

http://www.lancet2000.com

❑ ❑ ❑

Index

H

I

K

L

M

N

O

P

Q

R

S